Also by Nina Barrett

I WISH SOMEONE HAD TOLD ME

NINA BARRETT

THE

P·L·A·Y·G·R·O·U·P

SIMON & SCHUSTER

NEW YORK LONDON

TORONTO SYDNEY

TOKYO SINGAPORE

SIMON & SCHUSTER
ROCKEFELLER CENTER
1230 AVENUE OF THE AMERICAS
NEW YORK, NEW YORK 10020

DESIGNED BY PEI LOI KOAY
MANUFACTURED IN THE UNITED STATES OF AMERICA

1   3   5   7   9   10   8   6   4   2

LIBRARY OF CONGRESS CATALOGING-IN-PUBLICATION DATA
BARRETT, NINA.
THE PLAYGROUP / NINA BARRETT.
1. MOTHERHOOD—UNITED STATES. 2. WORKING MOTHERS—UNITED STATES.
I. TITLE.
HQ759.B286   1994
306.874'3—DC20   93-39170
CIP
ISBN 0-671-74710-X

TO "ANGIE," "GRACE," AND

"MARGARET," WITH THANKS

CONTENTS

IN THE KITCHEN

Angie's apartment is dark and melancholy, stacks of cartons piled neatly in the rooms, awaiting the morning and the movers, now less than twelve hours away. I am impressed that she has accomplished this much, but I have forgotten how much a person without a child *can* accomplish, and Angie has left Gabriel with his grandparents while she does this work. Still, I worry about her morale. Grace and I have come out tonight to help her because we are both nervous about the idea of her here alone in the compressed night hours, when the will tends to weaken and wild thoughts can multiply like cancer cells. Angie has been too vehement in her insistence that this sudden move to a desert city where she knows no one is *exactly* what is called for at this moment in her life.

Grace and I know this cannot possibly be true. For two years we have both listened as Angie tried to articulate the deep sense of frustration, restlessness, and despair into which she has been sinking ever since having a baby. We know how angry she is at her husband for liking his corporate job, for never being home, for acting as though he wished he were elsewhere when he *was* home; we know how overwhelmed she is by Gabriel's willfulness and energy, how close she is to the precipice of not being able to cope. No, Angie does not have the markings of the Resourceful Relocated Wife. She is not going to join the bridge club and the country club and the PTA, and entertain Jeff's business associates.

She is standing now in the kitchen doorway, holding out a stack of newspapers for Grace and me to use for wrapping up

the dishes. She has a hip new haircut, a boyish crop that
makes her small face look vaguely impish, except that her blue
eyes do not sparkle; they are tired, and they dart nervously,
restlessly, squirrelish, around the room, avoiding my gaze and
Grace's.

"I wish you guys would stop asking me if I'm going to be
okay," she says irritably. "It's like you're saying I can't handle
this."

Grace and I exchange a glance. "No, of course not," Grace
says slowly, in her precise, well-modulated way. "We don't
mean it in a mean way, you know. We're just concerned."

Grace stifles a yawn and cautiously lowers her great bulk
onto a kitchen chair. She is two weeks overdue with this new
baby, just as she was with the first, and she seems unnaturally
distended, full to bursting. She, too, looks tired. Her round
blue eyes have reddish rims and her straight brownish-blond
hair hangs limply around her face, which is swollen moonishly
with the water weight of pregnancy. She, too, seems edgy, and
I know from two years of listening to her stories that she is
scared of what is about to happen to her: the process of the
birthing of this baby, and whatever will follow from it.

"It's like what they used to always say at graduation," I say,
as cheerfully as I can. "You know: Commencement—not just
an end, but a beginning."

This is true for me as well, or rather, I will take advantage
of Angie's leaving to try to make it so. The metaphor pops
into my head that we are wrapping Angie's life up in layers of
newspaper, just as for two years we have been unwrapping the
layers of her life in conversation. I cannot resist this applica-
tion of closure. I have always loved graduations and good-byes
for the sense they give of life's forward motion: *We are done
now; we are free to move on.* And I am eager to close the book
on these past few years of my life, which in reality have had no
forward thrust at all, no narrative structure. I had a baby, I

lost my way, I muddled through, I had another baby; if you're reading for plot, you can stop here. But now, with Angie leaving, I can think that this odd detour into chaos and formlessness is over. The playgroup is ending; my need for a playgroup is ending. With my first book about to be published, I can see myself climbing back into the story of my life as I wrote it many years ago, and continuing on my way.

But for two years this playgroup was the only structure and drama in my life. No employer noticed whether I did or did not work, or paid me for (most of) what I did, or told me I worked well. No one fell in love with me; it sometimes seemed, on the contrary, that my husband might have fallen out. There was no community into which I fit; having babies had unfitted me to go most public places. But once a week, I went to playgroup.

Every Tuesday at three, we met in someone's apartment, and let the children run wild while we sat in the living room sipping herbal tea and letting out the stories that had accumulated inside us like parts of a massive jigsaw puzzle that had come without a master illustration on the box. We were all lost; we knew that much. We had each headed into motherhood confidently, with a clear vision of the master illustration in our heads; but somehow, whenever we spilled the pieces out and looked at them and tried to fit them together, they seemed to have come from some other, wrong puzzle. I began to think of our experience, privately, as Consciousness Lowering; for whereas those homebound women of the early seventies had sat around in groups envisioning a more politically just world based on the principles extracted from their discussions of personal problems, we were constantly measuring our lives by our received visions of political correctness. The personal was political, and there was no area of our personal lives that we could not analyze politically and discover ourselves to have fallen short, despite our best intentions. It was supposed to be okay to make a Choice to spend time with your children; and yet somehow it was not. Breasts filled, mouths sucked, breasts emptied, bellies filled, bellies emptied, diapers filled, diapers were changed, breasts filled. Later, peanut butter sandwiches were consumed, but the rest of the process was much the same. We could see the children growing with all this filling up, but by the standards by which we had been taught to measure ourselves, it seemed to us that all we got was emptier.

◈

An end, and a beginning. The embryo in the womb mimics the historical stages of human evolution, from single cell to shrimp to fetus, of which we are both the end and the beginning. The stories of humans are like that, too; if you view the cross section of a given moment in an adult life, you find the elements of all the stories that have gone into that moment, and all the stories that will come out. An expert in artificial intelligence, Roger Schank, argues that stories are the building blocks of our intelligence, as cells are the building blocks of our bodies. Everything new that happens to us is filtered through an enormous index in our minds containing the gist of all the other stories that have happened to us, and thereby achieves its meaning relative to those other stories.

I have always believed that Real Life occurs in stories, and that most of the best stories are contained in books rather than in Real Life. I have spent my whole literate life rooting through books by and about women, searching for the story I wanted to live in. After the playgroup broke up, in 1990, I ran across a book that explained, at least partially, why I had never succeeded. In *Writing a Woman's Life,* feminist scholar Carolyn Heilbrun compares the act of writing about a woman's life to the act of actually living as a woman. Both, she says, are difficult to do honestly, because there is so little honest precedent—so little honest plot. There is the old plot, where beauty is virtue and selection by a man for marriage the ultimate climax, and after that the story simply stops. There is a male plot, which has nothing to do with marriage, but rather turns on issues of independence and professional mastery or moral integrity, but women aren't supposed to use that one because it defines them, ipso facto, as unfeminine.

In the seventies, when I was coming of age, there was a great wave of feminism that tried to rewrite the old female plots to look more like the male plots. But, as anyone who has lived through adolescence understands, in the full force of rebellion one almost always ends up throwing the baby out with the bathwater. So there were certain issues that the stories that formed the building blocks of my intelligence simply left out, or treated as viciously as the old stories used to treat women who weren't beautiful or wholly good; and chief among them was the issue of wanting a baby. Motherhood does not fit very well into stories that are about independence and professional mastery or moral integrity, because raising small children is mostly about dependence and constant responsiveness to other people's needs and tolerance of chaos.

I didn't realize until the playgroup had broken up that I would want to write about it, and so I had no notes from that period with which to work. Instead I went back and spent days in front of a tape recorder with Angie and Grace, trying to reconstruct the events of those years and the older stories that lay beneath. My aim was not so much to create a journalistically literal account of that time as to re-create the essence of our conversations, our experiences, our interactions. There was something about that period in our lives that haunted me: the contrast between the way the culture at large seemed to regard staying at home to raise children—as a "luxury" that only a very privileged portion of upper-middle-class white women could afford, and that would automatically satisfy our most basic womanly desires—and the way we perceived what we were doing, which was struggling mutely through each day in exile from the world of grown-ups, where our contemporaries were presumably achieving all the things we had been raised in the feminist era to believe we must always be achieving.

As I tried to wrestle the events of those years onto the paper, I ran across another book that explained my difficulty. In *Composing a Life,* anthropologist Mary Catherine Bateson proposes another metaphor for the structure of women's lives. Rather than the linear flow suggested by the idea of a plot, in which ambition leads directly to goal (or the failure to achieve it), Bateson suggests that women by nature lead distracted lives, in which ambition is interrupted by childbirth, child rearing, love and the loss of love, the making of a home, and caring for relatives. Life is therefore an "improvisational art," and so "the individual effort to compose a life, framed by birth and death and carefully pieced together from disparate elements, becomes a statement on the unity of living. These works of art, still incomplete, are parables in process, the living metaphors with which we describe the world."

What that reminded me of, immediately, was the two quilts that hung on the walls of Angie's living room for the two years during which the playgroup met. There was the one she had made before having a child, when she first took a class in quilting. I thought it was beautiful: nine black squares, and in each square one of the two images she had designed herself, a flower with five petals and a pointy star that seemed to move around like a windmill when you looked at it hard.

But Angie said it was "corny." It was your basic textbook quilt, the kind of thing any old farm girl sitting in her kitchen would know how to do. A craft, not an art. Recently, her head had been exploding with ideas for really gorgeous quilts: big, wild designs that could not be contained within the patterns of any traditional quilt; bold, colorful shapes like paint spilled across a canvas. But whenever she tried to translate those ideas to fabric, she got stuck. Cloth was hopelessly inadequate for expressing her visions. It had been a long time, she said, since she had been able to finish anything, since she had been able to look at any one of her works in progress for more than a few days without being repulsed and shamed by her own lack of talent.

The second quilt that hung on her living room wall was another block quilt, but it was only half made. It hung there for two whole years with threads trailing off the unfinished bottom edge, while Angie remained suspended between the feelings she could not express and the medium of expression that was so inadequate. And it was hard, particularly in her case, to see this unfinished work as anything but a parable about the *dis*unity of that phase of all our lives.

There is only limited comfort in seeing one's life as a work in progress. Mary Catherine Bateson writes about a group of very high-achieving women. But for the rest of us, there is no guarantee that any object of beauty upon which we can gaze with pride will result; perhaps there will not be closure. It is much safer, really, to try to place ourselves in stories, where, knowing the beginning, we can try to predict the end.

CHAPTER 1

CHILDBIRTH STORY

G R A C E

There is no doubt that the history of childbirth can be viewed as a gradual attempt by man to extricate the process of birth from woman and call it his own. Indeed, some anthropologists and radical feminists believe that man has always been threatened by woman's exclusive power in childbirth, and that by placing his strength and intelligence against her docility and instinct he "won" an authoritarian role in society.

Suzanne Arms, Immaculate Deception: A New Look at Women and Childbirth in America

I can promise you control in labor. All you have to do is want it. If you are motivated to really want an unmedicated childbirth with a labor that is dignified and manageable, you can have it simply by listening to your breathing to ensure it continues in a calm, quiet, relaxed rhythm.

Susan McCutcheon-Rosegg, Natural Childbirth the Bradley Way

■　■　■

The apartment was ready. The refrigerator was stocked with juices and yogurt for quick energy in labor, and on the stove was the proverbial pot for boiling water. The king-size futon in the big bedroom had been made according to the doctor's instructions: one set of sheets, covered by a plastic sheet, with another old cotton sheet on top of that. After the birth, they would just peel off the plastic, and there would be a fresh, clean bed for Grace to sink into with the baby.

Grace's sister Kate had flown in from the West Coast just before the due date to attend the birth. In the past ten days they had binged on restaurants and plays, making much of savoring the last moments of Grace and Michael's freedom, but the merrymaking had dragged on a little too long, like a joke told twice, and by now, quite frankly, they were all getting antsy.

"There is no such thing as a late baby," said their childbirth books, "only a wrongly estimated due date." And in principle, of course, Grace and Michael agreed. But in reality, there was the fact that Kate's vacation from the symphony she played with had a limit, and her plane ticket had a return date; that Michael no longer got anything done when he went to work in the morning, expecting at any moment the call to Grace's side; and, above all, that even the philosophically committed home-birth doctor who was going to attend the delivery would insist on moving to a hospital if Grace were to fall into a medically high-risk category, for which going two weeks past her due date would automatically qualify her. And the name of the game here was: stay out of the hospital, at all costs.

Michael found himself explaining this over and over to his fellow graduate students in the political science department at Westerville University, who looked at him as though he were crazy for allowing this birth to happen at home. Michael was an extremely genial person, with a ready smile and a quick, smart-ass sense of humor, so you tended to peg him as a complete cynic and were rather surprised when in an apparently friendly conversation he suddenly whipped out his principles, hard, sharp, and nonnegotiable, and held them to your throat.

And the thing you just didn't get was that while you went around worrying about the dangerous things that *might* happen to a person who chose to have a baby unsupported by the medical expertise of a highly trained hospital staff, you were just buying into a system of medical propaganda that *totally overlooks* the dangerous things that happen every day to people *because* they put themselves at the mercy of a hospital staff, which unreasonably views every routine childbirth as a major medical emergency. And Michael would list the dangerous things for you, as did the books about the natural childbirth method that he and Grace had been studying: the routine use of drugs as painkillers and their unknown long-term effects on the baby; the interference with breast-feeding because of hospital policies and unsupportive nurses; the removal of the newborn to the nursery, which the founder of the Method referred to as the "Kid Concentration Camp," and the unknown effects of having the baby thus "incarcerated" on both the child and the mother's capacity to bond; plus a whole spectrum of potential complications due to medical intervention, including damage to the mother's tissues or the baby's brain from a forceps delivery, separation of the placenta, violent labor, amniotic fluid embolus, laceration of the cervix and birth canal, postpartum hemorrhage, uterine rupture, and fetal distress as a result of induced labor, not to mention the massive complications that could result from a cesarean section, which American doctors use with alarming frequency as a preemptive defense against malpractice.

If you really got him going, he might point out to you that most Americans live their lives in an absurd state of blind faith, trusting some nameless, presumably benevolent "Them" to take care of things. You walk into the supermarket assuming They have tested all the food additives to make sure they are safe; you take the drugs your doctor gives you assuming They have tested them to make sure any side effects will be negligible; and you assume They have tested your municipal water and determined it safe for drinking and tested your lake water and determined it safe for swimming and tested your air quality and determined it safe for breathing. Just as They tested Three Mile Island and Love Canal and Agent Orange, right?

Michael did not believe in Santa Claus or the Tooth Fairy, and he did not believe in Them, either. He hadn't since 1980, when, in his senior year at Harvard, he read the book *Diet for a Small Planet* and discovered that what Americans take home from the supermarket has almost nothing to do with good health and nutrition and everything to do with the profit imperatives of the food processing industries. Originally published in 1971, this book became one of the scriptures of the vegetarian movement and went on to sell more than 15 million copies. In it, Frances Moore Lappé makes an essentially simple argument: that it takes seven pounds of grain and soybeans fed to livestock to produce one pound of edible meat; that converting this grain into meat requires massive wasting of natural resources including water, energy, and topsoil; and that the food processing industries that make their money off this conversion process have yielded an American diet dangerously high in animal fat and protein, sugar, salt, additives, antibiotics, and pesticides, and too low in fiber. Why not, Lappé asks, skip the meat step and feed more people on a more healthful diet? This could happen, she says, if we voted with our consumer dollar. The political is the personal; we could cause an economic, ecological, and social revolution simply by buying, and refusing to buy. "[T]he only way that power will come to be more democratically shared," she writes, "is if you and I take more of it ourselves. If this is true, then the challenge to each of us becomes clear: we must make ourselves capable of shouldering that responsibility."

That was the same year Grace, at Georgetown, discovered Them in a women's studies class. One morning her professor walked in, opened a book called *Woman Hating*, by Andrea Dworkin, and began reading a description of the ancient Chinese practice of foot binding: how the toes of a girl of six or seven were bent underneath the sole of the foot and secured; how the bandage was wrapped around the heel to bring heel and toes together; how the bandage was pulled tighter and tighter month after month for years, until the foot had shrunk to the culturally erotic ideal of three inches, at which point the girl could no longer walk unassisted but would be highly desirable as a wife. "Mother would remove the bindings and wipe the blood and pus which dripped from my feet," the professor read, from a firsthand account in the Dworkin book. *"She told me that only with the removal of the flesh could my feet become slender."*

Grace thought, "That's awful, but we don't do that anymore." Then the professor asked, "How many of you have spent an entire day, let alone months or years on end, trying to conduct what you would think of as normal activity in a pair of ladies' high-heeled shoes?"

A student raised her hand and objected. "No one *makes* American women wear high heels. How can you be oppressed if you're doing something you freely choose to do?"

The professor raised one eyebrow and smiled, as though this were exactly the response she had hoped for. "But Chinese women also believed bound feet to be beautiful. It was the mothers, not the men, who carried out this gruesome and painful mutilation of their daughters' feet.

"The question," the professor continued, "is who sets the cultural standards for beauty, what purpose those standards serve for the people who create them, and what effect they have on the people upon whom they are imposed. In America, for starters, you have to look at who creates advertising, who designs fashion, who edits and publishes women's magazines."

Well, it was Them, of course. And They became one of the themes of the conversations Grace and Michael had been having since high school in Minneapolis, and were continuing to have long distance and during occasional long weekends in Cambridge or Washington. That was the same year, after four years of dating, they finally allowed themselves to have sexual intercourse, acknowledging that they were making a commitment to a joint future. Both raised in devoutly Catholic families, they had considered their long abstinence the best way of sharing responsibility to avoid a pregnancy they might not be ready to see through to the end. And now they were excited about this new way of shouldering responsibility for the adult lives they were just beginning. Public, political demonstration, as practiced in the sixties, was not the habit of this generation, but, just as Mary Catherine Bateson envisions a woman's life as a work of art, Michael and Grace saw that it would be possible to make of their life a work of politics. If eating meat promoted the exploitation of the earth and the unfair allocation of food resources, they would eat only vegetables. If throwing out their garbage endangered the environment, they would find ways to produce less waste and recycle what they did produce. If makeup and fashion were used to repress women's freedom and trap them in a pointless cycle of consumerism, Grace would dress simply and turn her real face to the world.

And so it was quite natural, seven years later, for them to see the act of childbirth as essentially political, and to try to head off the inevitable power struggle between technology and nature, between doctor and patient, between the Male Medical Establishment and the Sovereignty of the Female Body, by having the birth take place in their own home. The whole secret lay in educating oneself well enough to shoulder the responsibility instead of handing it to Them: You had to maintain control.

The night before Kate was booked to leave on a nine A.M. flight, the random warm-up contractions Grace had been having for weeks suddenly became very regular. The three were elated. Michael and Kate took turns escorting Grace up and down the hallway and through the living room, because the childbirth teacher had told them that if this was the real, serious thing, walking would help it along, and if not, the walking would stop it.

It didn't stop. All night long they marveled at the way Grace's great belly hardened and then softened in a slow, rhythmic pattern. And Grace remained so calm. Not that she was ever one to panic, or to give in to her feelings, or even to reveal them very much. She was always cool, but it was amazing that she could laugh and joke like this with such a momentous process taking place inside her body. Kate called the airline and switched her flight to two P.M., the last possible flight that would allow her to make her evening rehearsal. She was determined, having come this far, to see the baby born.

They were proud of how well they handled the first twelve hours of labor on their own, but when the midwife showed up in the morning, she found Grace to be only three centimeters dilated out of the necessary ten. The midwife did not seem at all impressed, and asked if she could lie down on the couch in the study; she had been up all night at another birth, and needed to get some rest.

Meanwhile, Michael noticed that Grace's normally impassive face had begun to register marked discomfort with each contraction. She didn't want to walk anymore. She complained of a shooting pain in her lower back that was growing stronger with each contraction and not disappearing in between, as did the pain of the contractions themselves.

"Back labor," said the midwife. The baby was posterior, she explained; it was facing Grace's front rather than her spine. "This kind of labor usually comes with a backache," she said, "but the baby will probably turn around on its own and then you'll feel a little better."

But Grace kept feeling worse. Michael was valiant, even relentless. The husband's role as labor coach was crucial to the Method, so there he was, rubbing her back, reminding her each time to let go of the pain.

When you are in labor yourself, you will want to picture the harmony of the work involved: the baby with built-in reflexes to help in birth, the uterus working in its designed way, and you, the skilled mother, relaxing at the right times with a supportive partner caring for you and coaching you through labor.

Something was very wrong. Michael could see he wasn't getting through to Grace; she wasn't visualizing harmony. Splayed out on the futon, she looked panicked, tormented, lost, like a very small boat bobbing up and down on top of a raging ocean. When she tried to change position, her face suddenly froze and she threw up on the bed. Then she sank back into the ocean, and he could not seem to reach her.

When the doctor showed up late that afternoon, she was still at three centimeters, and the baby hadn't turned, and she had thrown up again. The doctor waited a few hours, checked her again, and took Michael aside. "No change," he said. "I'm sorry, but I think we'll have to get her to the hospital."

Oh God, there it was. There was a saying in Michael's family: You go into the hospital for a splinter, and you come out with one less finger. There was a vaguely sadomasochistic image in one of the childbirth books, a reference to doctors who "*prefer to have every woman on a delivery table with her legs strapped into stirrups.*" Dr. Bradley, in his own book, describes the difference between a typical medicated hospital birth and a natural birth as "*the difference between being raped by a stranger and being loved by your husband.*" But they prepared you for this situation; that's why you took the course and did all that reading, that's why it was so important for the husband to be there, so when push came to shove, you wouldn't just hand the authority over to Them.

Michael faced the doctor. "Wait a minute," he said. "What do you mean, 'have' to take her?"

The doctor looked annoyed. "Look," he said, "she's been in labor all night and all day. She's exhausted and that's going to slow things up, and she can't eat or drink because she can't keep anything down, so there's a risk that she'll become dehydrated."

"So what can you do for her in the hospital that you can't do here?" Michael demanded.

"I can give her a painkiller and stop the labor temporarily so she can get one good night's sleep, so that maybe when she wakes up in the morning, she can get through the rest of it on her own. And we can get her some IV fluids."

Intervention, thought Michael. With every intervention, the heightened risk of a side effect or another intervention. He met the doctor's eyes. "What if we choose not to go?" he said.

The doctor returned his stare, coldly, and replied, "I'm afraid you really don't have a choice."

◈

They draped one of Grace's arms over the doctor's shoulders and the other over Michael's and half-dragged her down the stairs to the street, where she stirred briefly from the trance of her pain and threw up on the sidewalk. The doctor stopped the car halfway to the hospital so she could lean out the door and throw up again, retching uselessly now, for there was nothing left in her stomach but bile.

The medicated mothers vomited, something rarely seen in our method. . . . The mothers were actually sick from medication, but, from association, the mother's attitude toward the baby, subconsciously or even consciously, was "You make me sick."

◈

The hospital labor room was small, austere, uninviting. White-clad people appeared with wires and needles and belts and hooked her up. An electronic fetal monitor was strapped around her belly, to scribble out the magnitude of the contractions and the response of the baby's heartbeat on a huge, endless roll of graph paper. An IV needle was inserted in the back of her hand. And then came the bag of fluid—and the drug. Morphine. Almost immediately, the pain subsided. Michael curled up in a sleeping bag on the floor next to the bed and immediately sank into a deep, sound sleep.

But Grace could not sleep. Without pain, she now had room to think. To feel the contractions that were still rhythmically tightening and releasing her belly, not hurting now, but still marked enough to keep her awake. To wonder what this drug might be doing to the baby.

The drugged mothers' babies were dusky blue in color, unresponsive, listless, and needed to be aspirated or sucked out if mucus accumulated, because their muscles were too weak from the mothers' drugs to allow them to cough or clear their own throats. . . . We suspect mother medication to produce awkwardness instead of gracefulness in the baby's later life, shortened attention span and memory ability, inability to handle stress, impaired reading ability, hyperactivity, and probably many other subtle effects yet to be discovered.

To hear the hospital noises, the nurses talking in the hallway, the flush of the toilet in the shared bathroom, the coughs and moans floating down the corridors from other rooms. And the voice in her head, the echo of the promise of the childbirth text: *I can promise you control in labor. All you have to do is want it. . . .*

◈

Even as a little girl, she was always in control. She still remembered how careful she was in the big old Minneapolis house of her maternal grandmother, crammed with breakable things little kids could not touch or she would yell at you. When she meant to show affection, instead of giving you a hug, Grandmother was likely to give you a ten-dollar bill and send you down to the toy store to buy yourself a treat.

Grace and Kate, like twin Heidis with their long yellow braids and the frilly pink dresses their mother liked to sew for them, loved those occasions. They could stand for hours gravely and minutely examining the Hula-Hoops and the Easy-Bake ovens, the Funflowers you could make out of plastic Goop, the Barbies with extravagant hair and breasts and teeny-tiny waists (which their devout mother found morally reprehensible and would not allow in the house). So much choice, you felt rich just standing there with all of it before you. But they could never actually bring themselves to buy anything. It was fun to look, but spending money on those things seemed to the two girls frivolous and uneconomical, an unwise use of resources. So in the end they always took the money home and put it in their banks.

At Sacred Heart Elementary School, the girls were held accountable for their behavior at the weekly ritual of "primes." This was the ceremony for which everyone polished up the saddle shoes and then gathered in one room before the Reverend Mother. One by one, the girls were called to the front and handed a card on which was written either "Très Bien," "Bien," or "Assez Bien," according to their comportment. Then each girl made a ladylike curtsy to the Reverend Mother and returned the card to the box, vowing to be *plus bien* in the week to come.

Naturally, as a teenager, she rebelled—but carefully. After she got her first period, her mother had sat her down and lectured her about avoiding something she called the Near Occasion of Sin. What that meant was that you didn't go sit in the backseat of a car with a boy, because the temptation would be too great. Her mother did not hold the classic feminine Catholic belief that sex was actually unpleasant and its only purpose procreational; on the contrary, it clearly *was* enjoyable, and therefore the temptation was real and serious. But it was wrong, absolutely morally wrong to give in to it. And, from a purely practical standpoint, because abortion was completely unmentionable, it could ruin your life if you weren't careful. So you had to watch yourself every step of the way.

So in high school, when Grace made the sudden discovery that she was not the awkward, dank-haired, little-girlish self she thought she was, but a person in whom boys saw real temptation, she appeared to outsiders (such as her mother) to get alarmingly carried away. Sophomore and junior years, she must have dated twenty-five different guys, and of course she was doing all kinds of other things her mother wasn't even aware of, such as sneaking out of the house after she had supposedly checked in for the night; buying alcohol just to see if she could get away with it; seeing how much she could drink and still walk; making out in the basement, knowing that someone could walk in at any minute.

Was she out of control, or just out of her mother's control?

It was true that they couldn't talk anymore, that she sensed her mother always on the verge of anger, which is why she could never confide in her mother, which is of course part of the reason her mother, sensing what she was up to, was always on the verge of anger. But it was also true that Grace stayed up as late as necessary to complete her schoolwork, that she had a consistent A average, the highest in her graduating class, that she was coeditor of the student newspaper and highly active in the theater club at the Catholic boys' high school, where she met Michael.

And it was also true that through all the wild making out with all those different guys, she never once approached the line of the Near Occasion of Sin. She understood that intercourse was like those toys in the store when she and Kate had been little: It was out there and it was tempting but you had to want it badly enough to pay the price. And Grace did not.

And it was also true that when, after their whole senior year of dating, Michael decided he was feeling very much in love with Grace and decided to tell her so, there was an embarrassing little silence. She thought she was probably supposed to say the same thing back to him, and she liked him very much and didn't want to hurt his feelings. But how were you supposed to know that you *loved* someone? Wasn't there something that was supposed to run through your mind and body like a wild, raging flood? Was there something wrong with her, that she could only detect something more like a trickle?

It was many months before she glimpsed signs within herself, before she sensed that she was safe enough to say those dangerous words back to Michael. And then several years before they made the ultimate commitment and crossed over the line together into sin.

She was immobilized by the belts and tubes, like a beached whale in the bed with the high railings, and when she felt wetness spreading between her legs and realized the amniotic sac must have broken, she had no idea what to do. She didn't want to wake Michael. He had been up with her for all one night already, and she was going to need him in the morning. But no one ever came in to check on her. In desperation, she reached for the box of Kleenex on the bedside table.

◈

"What's all this?" demanded the nurse.

The room was flooded with sunlight, and Grace realized she must have drifted off, after all. Groggily, she followed the nurse's disapproving gaze down to the pile of soggy, wadded-up Kleenex on the floor next to the bed. "Oh," she stammered, "I'm, uh, sorry, but the waters broke and I didn't know how to call and I couldn't reach the trash."

"The button's right here," scolded the nurse, pulling out a gizmo that had been wedged between the mattress and the sidebar. Grace began to apologize again, but the nurse cut her off. "Someone will be in to check on you in a minute."

Then began a long parade of uniformed people—interns, residents, nurses, nurse's aides—Grace and Michael weren't sure who all of them were, and most of them did not introduce themselves, but simply walked in authoritatively and tinkered with Grace, as though she were a car being serviced. Her own doctor appeared midmorning, inserted a gloved hand into her vagina, and pronounced her to be, after thirty-six hours of labor, five centimeters dilated. Only halfway.

"I suggest we try Pitocin, to try to get things moving," said the doctor.

Grace gave Michael a desperate look. According to the

Method, Pitocin was a "second-rate copy of the hormone that naturally contracts the uterus." It could cause "violent 'tetanic' contractions which make the muscles contract all over at once"—just like "a big CRUNCH!" The contractions could cut off circulation to the uterus—and the baby's oxygen supply—"longer than nature intended."

"We'd rather not," Michael told the doctor. But he looked considerably more tired and less sure of himself than he had the day before.

◈

"What are you doing?" Michael asked the nurse, as she reached up toward the IV pole.

"I'm going to increase the dosage a bit," said the nurse, "as per your doctor's orders."

"I heard his orders," Michael said. "He told you to keep it between twenty-five milli-units and thirty-five milli-units, and it's already at thirty."

"But she's not progressing," said the nurse. "So I'm going to increase the dosage."

"You turn that sucker up without getting the doctor in here to look at her, and I'll call him up and get him here myself," Michael snarled.

The nurse shot him a look of pure scorn and strode out of the room. And it was another two hours before the doctor arrived to check Grace again.

◈

"You're at ten centimeters," said the doctor. "Congratulations. You're ready to push." Then he left.

Grace and Michael exchanged a look of weary triumph. It couldn't be long now, could it?

"Ready to push?" Michael asked.

"I don't know," Grace said weakly. "I don't think I have the urge."

You are examined and discovered to be completely dilated. Although you do not feel an urge to push, you will probably be instructed to start. Your doctor may have the clock running on you, so it makes sense to try pushing even without the urge as long as you are having contractions. Better this than to let the time run out (in the doctor's head) and have him wanting to intervene.

"I guess you should try pushing anyway," said Michael. It might have been prudent to ask the nurse for guidance, but the nurse seemed to be avoiding them. Grace's back was burning again, and she was trying to stay afloat in the fiery ocean. Where, when, how, was she supposed to push? Every few moments, she would tense up her muscles and try.

Noon. Forty hours of labor. There must have been a shift change, because suddenly the room was flooded with nurses. A big, authoritative-looking woman told Grace, "We think maybe you've lost a lot of your strength; you can't push hard enough. So we're going to help you along a little bit."

The nurse eyed the fetal monitor and waited for a contraction to peak. "Push," she yelled, and she and another nurse pushed down—WHAM—with their hands at the top of Grace's belly.

"This can't be right," thought Grace. She wanted to tell them to stop, but all she could manage was a moan. Push, WHAM, went the nurses. Push, WHAM.

Four in the afternoon. Forty-four hours into labor. The nurses had finally given up. Michael was still struggling along with the coaching, trying to talk Grace through the pushes her own body seemed uninterested in making, while she went feebly through the motions. Her face was white and spent, her hair hung damp and limp, and her eyes, when she opened them, looked wounded. When a nurse appeared to ask how things were going, she moaned, "I can't do this anymore."

"We're having another doctor come to take a look at you," said the nurse.

"Are they going to do a cesarean?" Michael asked. It was clear from his voice that the fire of his resistance had greatly cooled.

"I'd guess," said the nurse. "Maybe first they'll try forceps."

The list [of complications from cesarean sections] goes on and on. In a declining order of frequency it includes things like: hemorrhage, accidental re-opening of the wound, subsequent uterine rupture, injuries to adjacent parts of the body like the bladder or bowels, complications with blood transfusions including hepatitis, aspiration pneumonia, anesthesia accidents, and even cardiac arrest. Death occurs for the mother after cesarean surgery about once in every thousand operations. This is about ten times more often than in vaginal births.

"Just make it quick," thought Grace.

"Could you turn off the Pitocin, then?" she whispered hoarsely. The contractions were still mountainous.

"Oh, no," said the nurse. "We can't do that without the doctor's orders."

"Where's the doctor?" asked Michael.

"On his way."

In the operating room, almost an hour later, the anesthesiologist seemed to be poking around quite a bit at the base of Grace's spine. Michael could tell the exact moment when the epidural took effect. Grace's face, frozen for the past two days in a mask of misery and exhaustion, suddenly melted into a sort of blissful surprise. He had never seen an expression quite like that on her face, that deep, relaxed ecstasy. He hadn't realized how tense he himself had become until he felt his own face unknotting in response. This was not the way he had wanted the birth to end, but at least now it would be ending.

Then, suddenly, her face changed again. Her eyes went wide with terror, and Michael could see her mouth moving, though no sound came out of it.

"Stop!" he barked at the anesthesiologist as he made out the words Grace was trying to voice: "Can't breathe."

The world seemed to be stopping. This couldn't be happening, but of course it was happening; it was the thing they had feared from the moment the decision to come to the hospital had been made. He would leave here without a baby. He would leave here without Grace.

But the anesthesiologist looked calm. He bent over her, checking the dosage of the epidural, then bent down again to murmur in Grace's ear. "She's panicked, that's all," he said to Michael. "Normally, you lose sensation just below the waist, but she's lost it in the chest, and for a moment she didn't realize she was breathing. But she is breathing. She's doing just fine."

◆

After a few minutes, Grace could feel herself breathing again, and she began to relax. The anesthesiologist was very nice; he kept talking to her, soothing her, explaining why she'd had that sensation. Grace felt wildly, unreasonably grateful; he was the first person in the whole parade of hospital personnel who had recognized that she might be having feelings about this process.

She felt herself drifting off again into space and lightness, the incredible relief of the release from pain. Behind the curtain they had drawn around her lower body, she could feel some tugging, and then she heard a cry, and people seemed to be rushing around, and she heard someone say, "It's a girl," but none of this seemed to have anything to do with her. She wondered vaguely if something was wrong with it, but soon, Michael came over and he seemed to be smiling. He had a little bundle, but without her contacts in, Grace could only make out a little pink blur.

"They're sending her to the nursery for observation," Michael said. "Do you want me to go with her, or stay here with you?"

The length of time it took before the baby was put into the . . . mother's arms was directly related to lowered I.Q., depression, memory, inability to meet stress, attention span, and so on.

"I'll be fine," she murmured, although she could feel another big wave of nausea coming on. "You go with her."

So Michael left with the baby, just before they moved Grace from the table onto a gurney, and her stomach heaved and emptied itself one last time.

◆

"What's that?" Michael demanded of the nurse, who was about to squirt the contents of a plastic squeeze bottle onto his daughter's naked stomach.

"It's soap," said the nurse, who looked no more than seventeen.

"What are you going to use it for?" Michael asked.

"To wash her," said the nurse.

"Why don't you just use water?"

The nurse looked puzzled. "Because we always use soap."

"Well," said Michael, "this time, don't."

"I'm sorry," said the nurse, now annoyed. "But that is our procedure."

Damn their procedures. What is this strange woman doing with her hands on *his* baby, anyway, at exactly the point in this process when he and Grace and the baby should be left alone to experience themselves as a family?

"That stuff is *shit*," he snapped. "Why are you going to pour that stuff all over this poor little baby who was *just born*? You're going to take this *chemical stuff* that's got all these weird ingredients whose names you can't even pronounce and that are totally synthetic materials and you're going to rub it all over *my child*? FORGET IT!"

The nurse stood frozen for a moment, regarding him in amazement. Then she seemed to remember the baby.

Quickly, almost furtively, she squirted a small dab of soap onto the baby's stomach. But the dab was just a very tiny one, Michael noted with some satisfaction, and he accepted it as evidence that this final battle, at least, he had won.

◈

Grace spent six weeks flat on her back in bed because the anesthesiologist had accidentally punctured her spinal column in administering the epidural. Consequently, the fluid that normally cushions and protects the brain and spinal cord was slowly leaking out, and every time she attempted to sit up

or moved her head suddenly, she suffered an immediate, violent headache.

But even if she hadn't been virtually incapacitated, unable
to care for the baby, unable to do anything other than lie
there in what should have been the birth bed and run over
the whole birth experience again and again obsessively in her
head, she still probably would not have gotten around to calling the childbirth teacher to report in, as everyone in the
class had been asked to do. She knew exactly how that conversation would go.

But eventually the teacher called her and they had the
conversation anyway. First Grace related the facts, as neutrally as she could. Then there was rather a long silence, before the instructor said, "Oh." Then there was another long
silence, before the instructor asked, "Well, if you had to rate
your birth on a scale of one to ten, how would you rate it?"

Grace did not like this question. It smacked of market research, some statistic the teachers must have to report to
headquarters to prove theirs was the best possible childbirth
Method.

In the Bradley Method, when we say successful outcome, we
mean a totally unmedicated, drug-free natural childbirth without routine medical intervention that enables the woman to
exercise all her choices in birthing and give her baby the best
possible start in life. And we expect this over ninety percent of
the time.

On this scale, there was no question her birth experience
was a one, possibly a zero. She could tell from the instructor's
tone of voice that she was girding herself for a number that
was going to skew her statistics, possibly get her in trouble
with whomever she reported to. Wasn't it enough that Grace
had failed herself, and Michael, and baby Phoebe? Did she

also have to have this guilt of failing the childbirth instructor? Of being a woman whose body had not been capable of birthing a baby freely and naturally and thus standing up to the authoritarianism of the male medical establishment? Of having to go on the public record as saying, "The whole thing got totally out of hand; I just completely *lost control*"?

But Grace wasn't the type to let her anger and frustration out on a relative stranger, and certainly this poor woman should not be made to bear the consequences of Grace's personal failure, so she said, as diplomatically as she could, "I'm afraid I can't answer that question," and she thought the instructor sounded relieved, because of course that kind of reply wouldn't pull down the average, would it?

"The thing about you, Grace, is you tell this whole story about your childbirth and you tell everything except for how you *felt* about any of it. I mean, were you pissed off at the teacher? Were you pissed off at the hospital? Were you pissed off at Michael?"

Grace's expression, as she listened to the question, was half blank and half puzzled, as though she had only partially understood it but was still curious enough to entertain it. Angie's face, on the other hand, wore a look of intense concentration. I loved watching the two of them talk: Grace, who spoke and moved so softly, but kept her essential self as hard and impenetrable as an acorn, and Angie, like a hungry squirrel who had just gotten a treasure into its teeth and would gnaw excitedly until she cracked it open.

Before we began the playgroup, I had met Grace several times in the Tot Lot across the street from our apartment, the way you tend to meet the parents of children the same age as yours, particularly when they are fighting over a bucket and shovel in the sandbox, as they continually are. Sam and Phoebe, we quickly discovered, had shared a due date, though both had arrived late and, ultimately, five days apart. Now, at eighteen months, they were big, robust, rosy-cheeked toddlers, each with an incredibly fierce will. In conflict over a toy, each would grab an end and yell "MY" as loudly as possible until Grace stepped in and began to negotiate in her quiet, musical voice, which I always let her do because it seemed so much more thoughtful than my own instinctive response, which was to shout: "Guys, stop fighting."

But I never got much beyond the bare facts in these conversations, because Grace's answers tended to be guarded and almost monosyllabic, and I got the feeling that she was either way too cool or way too private to have the kind of orgy of mutual confession that I in my shell-shocked new motherhood was always seeking. All my life I had had close female friends who agreed that one of the great pleasures of existence was its minute analysis in intense three-hour conversations over food or diet soda or wine and cigarettes. These were the conversations that broke up Love, Sex, Betrayal, Parents, Careers, and Ambition into chunks small enough for adequate emotional digestion. That I had mastered this much of life already I considered to be not so much my own accomplishment as the result of a collaboration in which Mary Kuhn, Joan Herlihy, Mona Lisa Shallenberger, Vicki Tillen, Liza Collery, Marta Feldmesser, Cheryl Lambert, and my sister Joan Wickersham deserved equal credit.

But I had long since lost touch with or moved away from all of them, and for Motherhood I was on my own. Why couldn't I digest that? It wasn't even *on* the list of Life Events for which a close, analytical friend should be required. Love, Sex, Betrayal—these were the stuff of mighty literature and drama. But Motherhood wasn't on anyone's reading list; it seemed to happen after the story was already over, while everyone was living Happily Ever After in a life not requiring illumination or examination. (In feminist stories, it happened before the story began, and was the thing women had to avoid or become liberated from before the really interesting Personal Growth stuff could take place.) Possibly it was a sort of marketing problem: Motherhood, with its routine components of feeding, burping, diapering, etc., was supposed to be so dull and trivial that it had to be left out of literature and history altogether in order to avoid boring or alienating the consumers.

I had actually resolved, in my pre-baby state, that I would never make friendships based on feeding-and-burping talk. But I had vastly underestimated the loneliness of spending days in an apartment with a demanding infant, in a world where you were otherwise utterly out of context. I didn't know anyone in Chicago; my colleagues from journalism school—the reason my husband, Ellis, and I had moved there from New York in the first place—had graduated and dispersed across the country. I had no family in the area, and though I was attempting to establish myself as a writer, I was still in the ruthlessly demoralizing stage in which no editor ever returned my phone calls. There was no physical workplace to give me a sense of community, or even an ex-workplace full of ex-colleagues who might be curious to view the baby or quiz me with mixed pity and fascination about the story of my new life.

Therefore, in my post-baby panic, I realized I would have to relax my standards. And so I joined a new mothers' group in Chicago run by a Facilitator who encouraged us to talk about our Issues. The other women hesitantly ventured concerns about feeding and burping, while I desperately tried to drag in Love, Sex, Betrayal, Parents, etc. The Facilitator, who practiced Active Listening, followed up every one of our remarks by saying, "I hear you saying that you feel————," and then rephrasing the thing we had said so that it now sounded quite unlike the thing we had originally said. But we were all too intimidated or polite or bored or, in my case, frustrated to argue with her, and so the conversations tended to die quick little deaths.

So then I tried a new mothers' exercise class in suburban Westerville, where all the mothers came in color-coordinated sweat suits and laid their infants, in baby bouncers and Kangarockeroos, in a semicircle, while the instructor, who had notably enormous hips, played show tune tapes and improvised aerobics moves. The last fifteen or twenty minutes were spent exercising the babies by moving their arms and legs around as we sang about how the wheels on the bus go round and round and the wipers on the bus go "swish swish swish." Sam would start to scream every time I tried to put him down, so I never actually got any exercise. And there was quite a bit of burping-and-diaper talk and, needless to say, nothing much about Love, Sex, and Betrayal. But I didn't entirely give up hope until the day one of the women, who spoke in that kind of voice that is so sweet it comes out half sour, suggested that it was inappropriate for us to sing (after the babies on the bus went "wah wah wah" and the mommies on the bus went "ssh ssh ssh") that the daddies went "read read read." Because after all, fathers were actively parenting now, too, and we shouldn't perpetuate harmful stereotypes, and a more socially responsible lyric might be: "The daddies on the bus go 'I love you.'" And the women in the exercise class, including the instructor, were all too intimidated or polite or bored or, in my case, frustrated to argue with her.

By summertime, a little more than a year into motherhood, I was completely lost and lonely and had developed an almost physical sense of being on the verge of disappearing, especially in public places full of strangers. In the shiny, expensive Water Tower Place shopping mall in downtown Chicago, I suffered a panic attack in a crowded upscale deli. Dizzy, nauseated, gasping for breath, I felt suddenly that I was about to die right there, with Sam in his high chair on one side happily throwing wadded-up cheese bits and crumbled saltines onto the floor and on the other side two fortyish businesswomen in stylish suits discussing somebody's office affair. And I couldn't call for help because I wasn't sure I existed, not in the same universe as these purposeful people, who suddenly seemed to be very far away from me, so far that I was sure that if I shouted into the crowd, no one would be able to hear me.

That summer of 1988, the time was out of joint. By May the temperature was already shooting up into the high eighties, heralding the coming of the hottest summer ever on record in Chicago. That was the month a thirty-year-old white, upper-middle-class baby-sitter named Laurie Dann took a gun into a Winnetka elementary school, a few miles from our apartment, and shot six children, killing an eight-year-old boy. As the summer droned on, the temperature soared up into the nineties, then into the hundreds. Radio stations warned of dangerous ozone levels and cautioned the very young and the very old to stay indoors; but indoors there was no air, and the overwhelming demand for power to cool all the sweltering people caused frequent blackouts that silenced the fans and air conditioners and caused refrigerators to drip with the sweat of their rotting food. Millions of dollars' worth of crops withered in the dust. Old people and joggers dropped dead. In July a woman locked herself in the bathroom on a United Airlines flight from Newark to San Francisco for several hours, leaving it so splattered with blood that flight attendants closed it off for the rest of the trip; after the plane landed, a cleaning person found a crying newborn baby, its umbilical cord still attached, covered with paper towels in a cabinet beneath the sink.

The heat, the anxiety, the loneliness. There was no world to which I belonged. And yet I got up every day, wheeling Sam through morning after thick, stagnant morning toward the Lake Michigan beach, where I hoped the air might be a degree or two cooler. It was on one of those walks I first saw the two women, and their image lingered in my mind like a mirage in the quavering desert air: one light haired and one dark, pushing strollers side by side, intensely engaged in some conversation, their two pretty yellow-haired children trying to catch each other's hands across the gap between their strollers, shrieking with delight. The women seemed familiar.

They had the young, careless look of students, not the fussed-over look of suburban matrons clinging to their feminine allure, or the slovenly look of the ones who have already let go. They reminded me of me. But there were two of them, and though they smiled and waved at me as they passed, they seemed enveloped in the cloud of their own intimacy, like a perfume I briefly caught the scent of before it drifted by.

"If I had that," I thought as I trudged on, "I would be okay."

◈

After that, when I saw the light-haired woman in the Tot Lot with her big, cherubic daughter, I tried to start those conversations that never seemed to go anywhere. I was so discouraged by Grace's reticence that when I put the word out in September that I was starting a playgroup in my apartment to bring the whole Tot Lot crowd inside for the upcoming arctic months, I didn't even say anything to her about it. So I was surprised when I arrived home from the supermarket on the afternoon of the first playgroup meeting to find Grace's dark-haired friend standing outside my building, with her child in the stroller.

She immediately began to apologize. "Oops, I guess I'm early. And I guess you didn't exactly invite me, but I thought it would be okay, because someone said you were just asking everyone from the Tot Lot, and I was thinking of starting my own playgroup, but it seemed like if you were already starting one, it would just be easier to come to yours."

She didn't look very apologetic, though. She was smiling quite confidently, and her tone implied that of course she would be welcome, because we were both totally cool people. I was flattered by her air of familiarity. Her wiry son, Gabriel, had already climbed out of his stroller and chased Sam into the vestibule of the building. Angie followed me in, stood in my kitchen as I unpacked the groceries, and immediately confided to me that she was incredibly pissed off at her husband, and what was all this bullshit in the magazines about the New Dad?

As I shoved milk and eggs and cheese into the empty refrigerator, I nodded my head sympathetically, and smiled to myself at my great unexpected good fortune.

Many other women came to that first playgroup meeting, and some of them came back on an occasional basis afterward. But it was Angie, Grace (whom Angie brought with her the second week), and I who became the core of the group, the ones for whom Tuesday afternoon at three P.M. became a sacred and unbreakable commitment. As fall swept by, and the massive old elms of Westerville showered bright orange and yellow leaves into the streets, we ignored the glory of the crisp autumn days and hid out in my apartment, where the children spilled juice on my rugs, pulled leaves off my plants, chased our terror-stricken, pathologically shy Maine Coon cat, Raster, from closet to closet, and tore every toy and toy-fragment from its storage vessel. We tried to overlook everything short of hitting or crying, and sometimes they would disappear into Sam's room for whole blocks of minutes, leaving us free to discuss what Angie referred to as The Good Stuff.

"Like, if you bought a new car and the first week the muffler fell off, wouldn't you be pissed off at the dealer?" Angie persisted. "Wouldn't you call them up and say, 'You guys sold me a shitty car; I want my money back'?"

"But I don't think that's exactly the right analogy," said

Grace. "It's more like if you take a course where they promise to teach you French in six lessons, and you don't really learn anything, but at the end you're not sure if the problem was that they taught it badly or that you're just bad with languages."

"Well," I said, "it seems to me that their method should take into account that some people have more trouble with languages than other people. And childbirth methods never admit that. Or they admit it, but they make it sound like the women who have trouble have some kind of moral or sexual or willpower defect, so it must be *their* fault and not the method's."

"I read a book like that," said Angie, "where the writer compared birth to sex, because he said they're both about pleasure and pain and women have the same look on their faces when the baby's crowning that they have when they're coming, and they make little animalistic sounds."

There was a long pause while we all considered this. We could hear the kids in the sunroom, banging away at the toy drum and the xylophone on wheels that Sam usually used as a skateboard.

"The Bradley books were like that," said Grace. "They said there was something called a 'birth climax' that you could feel if you didn't have any drugs and you were sexually uninhibited."

"Oh, I see," I said. "So, you're supposed to maintain complete control, so that you can be completely relaxed and completely uninhibited."

Grace laughed.

"Yeah," said Angie. "It's like growing up Catholic in America. Your whole life, you hear about how it's the woman's responsibility to be in control and not let stuff get out of hand, and then one day watching *Oprah* you find out that it's the women who let everything get out of hand who are sexually well adjusted and having all the fun."

"My own theory," I said, "is called the Cyclical Generational Disillusionment Theory. You know how they keep making all these war movies where the idealistic young boy goes off to fight a war and become a Man, but then—shock of shocks—he discovers that war is full of blood and cruelty and *killing* people? That war is BAD? Well, I think women are like that about childbirth."

"But what about childbirth teachers?" said Angie. "They've mostly had kids already; they should know what it feels like."

"Who knows? I mean, there are army officers who know war is about death and slaughter and tortured babies and they still go back for more. There's a war type. Childbirth teachers are women who just happen to be good at childbirth, but they chalk it up to the Method and their own personal willpower, instead of just thanking their lucky stars, and then they join this cult that insists it has The Answer for everyone."

"I take it you had an unsatisfactory experience yourself," said Grace.

"Let me put it this way," I said. "My Lamaze teacher, who was pregnant with her fourth kid, came in one night with a chart entitled 'The Four Stages of Labor.' Under the heading were four smiley faces, one for each stage. In 'Prelabor,' the face was actually smiling. Under 'Labor,' it looked a little stunned. Under 'Transition,' it was grimacing a little, with two little beads of sweat flying off its face. And then in 'Pushing,' it just looked kind of goofy and out of it."

"Well," said Grace, smiling, "it certainly does sound as if she had very easy labors."

"But see, I've been researching this quite a bit for the book I'm working on now, and I know for a fact that most women don't. And those smiley faces have been bothering me for a long time, because I get the feeling it's all part of the same—I don't know what the right word is, 'conspiracy' makes it sound too orchestrated, but it's part of the same thing in our society that trivializes everything about motherhood and makes it out to be dear and sweet and dumb. If *I* were illustrating childbirth, I would show a naked woman standing at the very edge of the world, alone, in front of some huge, angry, fire-breathing god."

Angie laughed and said, "Your Lamaze class would get lousy word-of-mouth."

But Grace suddenly looked as though a dislocated joint had just popped back into place. "Not a god," she said, "but a goddess. And the conspiracy you're talking about is called patriarchy."

"MY!" There was a small shriek in the sunroom, the distant rumble of an oncoming thunderstorm, and I saw Grace glancing toward the children. I spoke quickly, because I thought we might be onto something and I didn't want her to get up and leave.

"But, Grace, that's too politically correct. That's wishful thinking. It *should* be a goddess, and many years ago it probably *was* a goddess, but today it's a god, and that's why childbirth is so humiliating, because you do have to stand totally naked and humiliated before it."

"That's exactly what feminists and natural childbirth advocates have been trying to fix," said Grace. "They've been trying to get childbirth back for women."

Another shriek from the sunroom, louder this time.

"But they go about it all wrong," I insisted. "They took a political issue and turned it into a personal issue. Instead of going out and lobbying the American College of Obstetrics and Gynecology to change the way hospitals handle birth, or promoting the spread of midwifery, or encouraging more women to become obstetricians, they put all the pressure on individual women to work out the power struggle through their own bodies. And that's why we both feel so bad about it now, because it wasn't just a painful experience we went through, it was a grave moral failure."

"The thing you said about midwives is true," said Angie. "I had a shitty experience, too, two days of this incredibly painful labor and then a C-section, and I came out looking like a battered wife, but the whole time I had this woman Paula sitting there, holding my hand, and she wasn't screaming at me to control myself, she was just saying, 'You've got to try to go with it,' and after the C-section she kept telling me it wasn't my fault, I did everything I could."

"But that's just what I mean," I said excitedly. "There's this whole male way of looking at the world that says, 'You have to control yourself at all costs.' And the feminist women's health people bought into that rhetoric and applied it to a situation where it doesn't work. Just like that whole seventies feminist idea that you must have complete control over your career and your income and your love life and dress in a suit like a man and act like a man and think like a man and play by all their rules—" I could hear my voice suddenly, surprisingly, start to crack and I knew I was at the very edge of tears, but I couldn't stop. "And if you grew up believing in that and having those ideas and values and then you have a baby, you find out that it just doesn't *work* that way."

"AAAAAAAAANNNH" came an undeniable loud wail from the sunroom, and all three of us rose in unison. Gabriel was standing with Sam's plastic drum strapped around his shoulder, his face red and contorted with grief. Next to him stood Phoebe, looking very innocent and bewildered, holding the yellow plastic drumsticks. Sam was over in the corner with one foot on the xylophone, so it looked as though I were off the hook this time.

Angie put her arms around Gabriel. "Were you using the drumsticks?"

Gabriel, still sobbing, nodded.

"Phoebe," Grace said musically, "please give back the drumsticks."

Phoebe clasped the drumsticks to her chest and shook her head vigorously.

"Wasn't Gabriel playing with them?" Grace prompted her.

Phoebe shook her head again and hugged the drumsticks closer.

Grace glanced at Angie for a cue. Angie's face looked wounded, and she was rocking Gabriel back and forth on her lap, crooning to him, not looking at Grace. Tot Lot etiquette mandated that the mother of the transgressor was usually responsible for solving the conflict, and the mother of the victim merely waited observantly for justice to be done. In conflicts over sharing, you had to understand what was proprietary and what was public domain. If your kid brought a squirt gun to the park, for example, that was a "special toy," and your kid had a right not to share it, and a kid who picked it up had to be convinced by his mother to leave it alone. (In Westerville, you might also then overhear her pointedly remarking to another mother how surprising it is when parents allow their children to play with toys that promote violence.) But in the sandbox, anything you brought but weren't actually using was fair game for anyone else, and a child who wanted to hold on to all of his shovels when someone else needed one would have to be lectured about sharing. It reminded me of conversations I had with my single New York friends, who all had therapists: Life was about boundaries, and knowing which ones were flexible and which ones you had to respect. I guessed this was how you learned it, whether from what the grown-ups told you or what you actually observed them doing among themselves; and sometimes you could see that the parents hadn't quite got it ironed out.

"Did you just want to touch them?" Grace asked Phoebe, as

Gabriel cried even louder. "Sometimes she just wants to touch something," she added apologetically and, I thought, a little pleadingly, to Angie. "Listen, Phoebe, you can hold them for a count of five, and then you have to give them back to Gabriel, okay? One . . . two . . . three . . ."

"WAAAAAAAH!" went Gabriel.

"Four . . . five. Now, give them back, please."

Phoebe shook her head hard and hid the drumsticks behind her back.

"Phoebe," said Grace, "if you don't give them back yourself, we're going to have to go into the other room and have a talk."

"NO!" shrieked Phoebe, and then, when the sticks were pulled from her hands, she too burst into tears. Grace picked her up, red and screaming, and carried her into the third bedroom, which I used as my study.

Angie and I went back and sat down on the couch. Gabriel was fine the moment he had the drumsticks back, but Angie still looked pale and a little frightened.

I tried to think of something to say to ease the tension. "It's funny, sometimes, how badly they want something that looks so insignificant to us."

"I don't think it's funny at all," Angie said. "When they start to scream like that, I know exactly how they feel."

CHAPTER 2

MIND-BODY STORY
N I N A

For women who wish to live a quest plot, as men's stories allow, indeed, encourage, them to do, some event must be in-
vented to transform their lives, all unconsciously, apparently
"accidentally," from a conventional to an eccentric story.

Carolyn Heilbrun, Writing a Woman's Life

■   ■   ■

Every morning for the past fifteen years I have ringed my eyes
with black eyeliner before facing the outside world. Otherwise, I'm not much of a makeup wearer, and actually used to
be against it on feminist principle, until my freshman year of
college. That fall I had a brief but emotionally intense involvement with a young man who did not approve of women
wearing makeup on the grounds of its being fake. Which was
of course one of the opinions for which I adored him, until he
suddenly broke things off for reasons I did not entirely understand. Somehow, in my furious determination to prove both
to myself and to him that I didn't need him anyway, I ended
up at the makeup counter in Lord & Taylor outlining my eyes
with kohl.

I am still against makeup on feminist principle, on the
grounds that the industry makes a fortune convincing women
that their natural faces are inherently flawed. On the other
hand, I trace my own addiction to eyeliner not to a desire to
attract a man but to a desire to rid my heart of one, and I still
feel a little kick of resolution every time I apply it, as a smoker
feels the little kick of nicotine on the initial drag.

I only mention this now to illustrate how complicated the definition of "feminism" has become for me—and many other women—these days. Is it about independence of individual action, in other words, personal choice? Or adherence to a preconceived set of political principles, in other words, political correctness? When I read the writings of the older generation of feminists, I'm often simultaneously impressed by my deep agreement with the essence of the arguments they make and by the ironic divergence of the actual choices I have made in my life; but then I think, one woman's conformity is another woman's rebellion, and every woman's quest begins with the collapse of her personal expectations.

◈

I can remember the exact moment I fell out of my story. It happened one dreary mid-January day in 1987, in the career advisory office of the Medill School of Journalism, when I was seven months pregnant. I had just finished work on my master's degree in December, and I was there for a job interview with *The New York Times*.

"Now remember," joked a friend who was scheduled for the interview after mine, "he's not legally allowed to ask you if you're pregnant."

We both laughed. I had already put on thirty pounds and my gray wool maternity jumper stretched tight across the mountain of my belly; I looked as though I might be about to go into labor any moment. I hadn't given this fact much thought in regard to the interview. In my last quarter at Medill, I'd been running all over the city of Chicago interviewing people for news stories and, far from being an obstacle, my belly had been functioning as a handy conversational icebreaker.

As I steered it into the interview room, however, it became almost immediately apparent that on this occasion my belly was going to be the iceberg that sunk the *Titanic*. After a fleeting expression of shock, the interviewer, a white man in his early fifties, composed his face and proceeded to address my stomach: "So, tell me why you are interested in working for the *Times*."

It was clear as I talked, however, that he wasn't remotely interested. He didn't ask any questions. He didn't meet my eyes. He did deliver a little lecture about what the *Times* expected from its young copy clerks, which, he kept reiterating, was very long hours and total commitment. His tone implied that I had probably misunderstood this, and that once he cleared up the misunderstanding, I'd get up and thank him and apologize for wasting his time. Instead I kept desperately asking *him* questions because it was the only way I could think of to insist that I was taking this seriously, and so should he. "Well, we'll let you know," he said finally, glancing at his watch and escorting me to the door, and I bit my lip to keep from saying, "I think you already have."

"They're famous for their arrogance," my friends consoled me afterward. But they had prescreened my résumé, so I knew I couldn't have been utterly out of the ballpark. At least on paper. And I had spent most of my life getting into elite institutions, including Andover, Yale, and Medill, so I was positive, thinking it over, that it couldn't be a problem with what I looked like—on paper. As for what *I* looked like—well, I suddenly realized I thought of "I" primarily as being my mind. I had always measured myself by work, first in sixteen years of school, then in book publishing, then in journalism, so wasn't I actually an identity that existed most *really* on paper? I had spent so many years of my life in male institutions, playing male games by male rules, often dressed in male clothing, that I had forgotten that my mind was attached to a physical form

that could betray me at any moment by sending out the signal
that allowed men to ridicule or disqualify me: that I was, in
fact, a woman.

❖

In 1971, when I was eleven years old, my parents decided to
take me out of the public school in the rural Connecticut
town where we were living and enter me instead in private
school. The private school was a boys' boarding school that
had only recently begun taking in girls as day students. The
year I started, there were 150 boys and 4 girls.

The school itself was lovely, a series of low white buildings
sprawling off from the Main House, which had once been a
private mansion. It was set in the rolling Connecticut coun-
tryside, with rich green playing fields stretched out to the
woods in back and a running track that wrapped around a
scenic tree-lined pond off to one side. It was affiliated with
one of those somber New England Protestant sects and actively committed to instilling proper morality in its boys, who
ranged from fifth graders up to ninth and seemed to be there
mostly because of learning disabilities or mild behavioral
problems, or because their wealthy parents had other priorities in life.

The attitude toward girls in the school community was
markedly ambivalent. Although we were sent every Wednes-
day afternoon to the headmaster's mansion to drink tea and
make polite chitchat in the solarium with the headmaster's
wife, we were also expected to attend school assembly every
morning and recite, along with the boys, the prayer that
ended with a plea to God to help us become "more of a man
each day." Neither the chitchat nor the prayer availed me socially. Skipped from fifth grade into seventh because of my

test scores, I was a prepubescent brain adrift in a sea of raging male hormones, and I came unequipped with traditional female flotation devices. The other girls seemed to know instinctively how to flirt; I knew instinctively how to compete. I withdrew into myself and studied my way to the top of my classes. The boys sidled up to me in the hallways, sneering, "Hey, Nina, are we still lovers?" and "Hey, Nina, I like your booooobs." One boy followed me around asking lewd questions about the female anatomy, humiliating me into speechlessness, until one day when he wondered, in his leering southern drawl, if it was true that I wore "tam-POONS." I stared at him a moment until I realized his mispronunciation was ignorant rather than malicious, and then dissolved into such gales of derisive laughter that he beat a confused retreat and thereafter left me alone.

I do not remember whether my parents were aware of how miserable I was during those two years; if they were, it must have seemed to them that I was getting something called an Education which would make all the misery ultimately worthwhile. I remember that my only source of hope and comfort at that time came not from home or from school but from a faraway world that existed only on television and in the books and magazines my mother read. In the great outer world, a feminist revolution was sweeping the country, addressing the problems women encountered in life simply because they were *female*. The Senate was passing the Equal Rights Amendment, which would prohibit discrimination against women; a new form of address and then a magazine—Ms.— were born, to insist that a woman's identity encompassed more than her marital status; Betty Friedan was a regular heroine of the media, proclaiming that now was the time that women would begin to make "policy, not coffee!"; and Billie Jean King was playing Bobby Riggs at tennis.

The battle of the sexes was my everyday element, and so I

took Women's Lib immediately to heart, and used it as my inspiration and the key to my resistance. I began by refusing to say the last line of the daily prayer in assembly. The assistant headmaster noticed and gave me a disapproving look, but when nothing further happened, I began to boycott the entire prayer. After all, I reasoned, I wasn't just a libber, but an atheist libber.

One day my eighth-grade English teacher assigned a class debate on the topic "Men Are Superior to Women, or Vice Versa." We were allowed to choose sides, which instantly set me against eleven boys. One of the faculty wives, who did arts and crafts with the girls in the afternoons while the boys went off to sports, encouraged me to make the argument that all embryos start out anatomically as girls; she had just had a baby, so she had done some reading, and she assured me that the penis was a mere afterthought of fetal development.

That sounded fine to me, except that I didn't see how I could possibly get up in front of the eleven boys and say the word "penis." At the time, my impression of a penis was of a slimy, uncontrollable thing that made males deeply perverted (as it was clear, at that school at least, they were). As long as men walked around in their clothes, hiding it, it was possible to pretend that they didn't have it, and therefore that they were normal, decent human beings. But to say the word—to suggest that eleven penises actually lurked right there in my English class (twelve, counting Mr. Hunter's) underneath eleven innocent pairs of corduroy and khaki slacks—would have been outrageously rude, like pointing to a person in a wheelchair and screaming, "You are crippled!" Surely, after that, we could never return to the diagramming of sentences.

I no longer remember what argument I used, except that I spent hours in the library researching it. The boys' team, on the other hand, did no research at all. Research, they felt, would have demeaned them. It would have suggested that *evi-*

dence of male superiority was required, when actually this fact was apparent, a priori, to all.

So I won the debate easily, at least according to the teacher. But about a week later Margaret Court played that first, highly publicized libber-versus-male-chauvinist-pig tennis match against Bobby Riggs, and lost. The boys in my English class were ebullient. Here it was, empirical proof! Her boobs had gotten in the way of her swing; it must have been "that time of the month"; and on and on. I sat in my seat, trying to make myself deaf. It didn't matter how much research I did; they outnumbered me, so they would always decide what constituted superiority, and what constituted proof. And it didn't matter how careful I was to respect the privacy of their embarrassing penises; they would always feel free to relentlessly ridicule my "boobs." Mr. Hunter, sitting on one corner of the desk with his arms crossed over his chest, made no attempt to control the class. When I looked at him, desperately, he gave a me a little wink, as if to say "Boys will be boys." He did call after me, though, as I got up and walked toward the door. He came out into the hall several times during the forty-minute period to try to get me to come back in, first by cajoling me, next by warning that I was about to flunk Conduct, and finally by threatening to send me to the headmaster. But I had already learned the lesson of the day. I knew I couldn't win, but I had nothing to gain by surrendering except collaboration in my own humiliation.

PENISES AND BOOBS

CHICAGO—Penises and boobs, penises and boobs. Underneath all the carefully crafted, passionless language of the feminist scholars who write about sexual harassment, this is what it boils down to. For a long time after women flooded the workplace in the 1970s, we worried about how they could Dress for Success, i.e., cover up the boobs as well as business suits have camouflaged the penis; perhaps we should have tried to reintroduce the codpiece, in variable sizing. But now, here I am at this job interview with this great undisguisable third boob, the Mother of All Boobs, and if the first two came stamped with a warning sticker (and what would the warning sticker say, anyway: "Handle with Care: This creature may be sexually active" or "Beware: This creature may remind you of your mother, about whom you have mixed feelings"?), this third one clearly comes with an equally severe deterrent: "Warning: This potential employee may have other priorities."

◈

I left the little boys' school at the end of my eighth grade year in what seemed to me at the time to be triumph: clutching an engraved silver cup awarded for the top academic performance in the graduating class. Only a very long time afterward did I understand that the price of the triumph had been that the school had succeeded, despite my resistance, in Building my Character—that I had, in fact, become "more of a Man each day."

I went on as a day student to another nearby boys' prep school that had recently gone co-ed, where I was academically bored and still socially withdrawn and spent a great deal of my time reading my way through the library. I read eclectically. Having discovered the *Iliad* and the *Odyssey*, and stumbled on the dramatic story of how Heinrich Schliemann had actually gone and unearthed Troy exactly where the old stories said it would be, I had resolved to become an archaeologist, and was studying ancient Greek and Latin. I knew the history of every English monarch from the Plantagenets to James I, and the names of all six wives of Henry VIII in order, and in addition to the authorized Desmond Morris version of human evolution, which was assigned for freshman biology, I knew the feminist revisionist Elaine Morgan version, which was not. I discovered a series of Suburban Novels that offered intriguing clues about what might be going on beneath the surface of my own outwardly perfect but ominously muffled home life: *Mr. Bridge, Mrs. Bridge* and *The Man in the Gray Flannel Suit* portrayed the emptiness and futility of the middle-class American Dream, where the man does something dull and demeaning so the wife can lead a dull and demeaning life among her high-status possessions, and their children, burning with genuine passion, grow up to hate them. And then there were the Women's Novels my mother read, a genre that continued to grow throughout the years in which I came of age, gaining momentum and credibility as the seventies rolled along: *Diary of a Mad Housewife, Memoirs of an Ex-Prom Queen, Fear of Flying, How to Save Your Own Life*, the resurrected nineteenth-century novel *The Awakening*, which became a basic feminist text, and culminating, in 1977—the year I started college—in *The Women's Room*.

The Women's Novels created in my mind a strong impression of the shape of a woman's life that I carried with me all through my teens and twenties, and that was this: In the Old Days (the fifties, when most of the authors of the Women's Novels had come of age), there were Bad Girls and Good Girls. Bad Girls got their lives ruined because they gave in to male sexuality and lost their reputations and no good man would marry them, or they got pregnant and had to have the baby, or they got pregnant and died having a botched abortion. Good Girls got their lives ruined because they resisted boys' sexuality and therefore repressed their own, until they got married and got pregnant and frittered away all their energy and ambition and repressed sexuality trying to raise impossible, ungrateful, spoiled children, while their husbands went out and had affairs and ultimately abandoned them for younger women. The solution—which Liberation had achieved for us—was total independence, meaning that women fully expressed themselves sexually through premarital, extramarital, postmarital, or instead-of-marital affairs, fully expressed themselves intellectually through stimulating careers, and left or divorced their mates at any sign of resistance. The impossible, ungrateful, spoiled children pretty much disappeared from the equation, or at least no one seemed to worry about them, least of all me. I was one myself, and saw little charm in the idea of ruining my own life for the sake of producing more.

It would be hard to imagine a message more perfectly tailored to the needs of a thirteen-year-old girl who now believed that her body was the source of all humiliation and her brain the means of her salvation. It left me free, as I plodded through the dull routine of my real life, to fantasize a future in which I would excavate lost palaces or observe primates in the bush or point telescopes at the stars. I didn't worry about the sexual expression part. There was an exquisite feeling I already knew about that could happen in my body when I was by myself, but I didn't associate that with sex, because I thought sex was something you had to have with a boy, and I frankly couldn't imagine meeting an actual boy I would want to have it with, or a desirable one who would actually want to have it with me.

So naturally I was not prepared when, in the spring of my first high-school year, I inadvertently landed a very big catch. It seemed that way, anyway, since it was the guy my best friend had had a crush on from afar all year. I had spent a lot of time consoling her because he was so far out of our league, so cool, so nonintellectual, so arrogant, so . . . blond. I didn't especially like him. However, here he suddenly was, hovering around me in the library lounge, where the day students hung out, inviting me for long walks in the woods in back of the school, and, after weeks of the shiest, subtlest overtures, gently kissing me, his hand on the back of my neck, trembling. Just thinking about it the next day made something deep within my belly tighten with excitement.

He had his hand inside my bra by the time summer vacation cut short our exploration. How could I go the whole summer with my body extinguished, when I now understood it was meant to have this electrical current running through it, which was produced by the male? But he lived fairly far away and wouldn't be eligible for his driver's license until he turned sixteen in the fall; therefore, our parents would have to drive us back and forth, something we both instinctively wished to avoid. One day, he promised, he would get on his bike and make the very long ride over to my house, and we'd hang around at my swimming pool.

Oh God, he was going to see me in a *bathing suit*. That, I understood, would be a disaster. My body could not withstand that kind of exposure. My body did not look anything like what I understood a normal female teenage body to look like. I had the kind of body that would have made some hearty Ukrainian peasant man happy. It was a sturdy work-horse kind of body, not that high-strung thoroughbred kind of body I saw in women's magazines and in movies, with all the visible bone structure: the high cheekbones with hollows underneath, the protuberant collarbone, the slightly concave belly framed by two prominent hipbones, the minimalist breasts, no more than a pair of pointy nipples, that looked so good in the politically fashionable braless style, under clingy shirts.

Well, this, the magazines assured me, I could control. I would simply have to lose ten pounds, preferably twelve. I set about it in the same quiet, determined manner I had studied my way to the top of the class. I read my mother's diet books cover to cover and memorized the calorie charts in the back. I cut out pictures of the boniest models from the magazines and pasted them into a scrapbook for inspiration. Then I stopped eating.

And I discovered that I was good at it. In the diet books, there were lots of stories of backsliding and complaining, lots of exhortations to continue despite the fact that one would feel continually deprived and hungry. But that, I thought, was like how you had to work very hard in school if you weren't very gifted naturally. I was naturally gifted at dieting. I didn't feel deprived at all, I felt a great rush of energy and enthusiasm, a sense of being hugely challenged every day and hugely gratified when I met each challenge. I didn't feel hungry, in the sense of having an appetite, of interpreting the sensation of hunger as a cue to eat. To me, hunger became its own reward, the sign that my goal was coming quickly closer, a sign that my body was consuming itself: *Only with the removal of the flesh could my body become slender.*

At the same time, I became obsessed with food. Each night as I lay in bed, I planned the next day's minimal menu, going over it and over it, adding the calories, trying to engrave the total in my mind, brainwashing myself to ensure that my intake would be fully programmed and not subject in any way to whim or failure of will. I might also fantasize about something I was going to cook. The only books I read now, besides diet books, were cookbooks; it didn't cost, after all, to *look.* Sometimes I acted out my food fantasies, in the manner of a voyeur, producing elaborate linzer tortes and braided dinner rolls and three-cheese soufflés, which I would not touch myself but would set before the family. And it was not their pleasure that I relished, watching them eat, but their weakness, which only highlighted my own strength. I kept track of their intake as well as my own, calculations running constantly in my head, my calories subtracted from their calories, an exact arithmetic of my virtue and self-control, more absolute than any school report card.

When I had lost the twelve pounds, I felt ready to consummate the swimming date. But it was a week before my friend could come, and I was having some trouble stopping the diet, so by then I had actually lost fifteen. I was trembling with excitement as I unveiled my bikini-clad form before him, but he did not seem to comprehend the momentousness of the occasion, and simply dived into the water. Later, we went into the crumbling barn behind the house and made out, but now his lips on mine seemed wet and rubbery, his tongue thrusting and invasive, his hands hot and clumsy on my body.

◈

We did not speak to each other again that summer, or after school began again in the fall. I continued to lose weight; then I stopped menstruating. After school began, my friend who had originally had the crush on him reported, "He's worried that you're sick or something. He says you bent over to put some books away the other day and he could see the whole outline of your spinal cord through your shirt."

Well, it wasn't boniness, exactly, but surely a visible spinal cord was as sexy as protuberant hipbones. Why, then, wasn't he still hanging around? My friend reported a little later that *she* had heard from a friend of hers that he had felt I "wasn't coming along fast enough."

"You're kidding," I gasped. "You mean he actually thought I was going to *do it* with him? He thought a fourteen-year-old girl was going to *do it?*"

A month later, just before Thanksgiving, she reported further that the friend of hers who had passed this information along was now going out with him. And they were Doing It.

◈

That night I couldn't sleep. I kept thinking about graham cracker piecrust. I had been planning to make a chocolate cream pie for Thanksgiving, mostly so I could scrape the chocolate and whipped cream off my piece and just eat the crust. I began to fantasize about that crust, how satisfying it would be in my mouth, how heavy and crumbly and sweet.

I slipped out of bed and crept quietly downstairs through the darkened house to the pantry. The store-bought piecrust was there in its tin pie pan, protected by a plastic sheath. I crouched down on the floor of the pantry in my nightgown, ripped off the plastic sheath, and began to cram greedy handfuls of piecrust into my mouth. It tasted rich and wonderful. I knew what I was doing was disgusting, but I couldn't stop myself: I was hungry. When I finally crawled back into bed, there was a slight hill between my hipbones, where I had so arduously carved a valley. I was full and drowsy. My parents had recently offered to send me to boarding school for the last two years before college, as they had sent my older sister to Exeter. I hadn't been sure, but now, as I drifted off to sleep, I suddenly knew: I wanted to go away, to somewhere I could start life over again, from scratch.

THE HUNGER

CHICAGO—Where did this pregnancy come from, anyway? Feminist Life Principle #1 is, Control your fertility. And anybody could tell you, the final six months of graduate school is not an optimal maternal moment for the ambitious, modern overachiever interested in prestigious job opportunities. But this was when I began to feel the hunger gnawing at my belly. I was married to a man I loved, a gentle, funny, warm man who felt like family, and suddenly for the first time in my life the women at the beach with two small kids made me more envious than the women with their lovers, and I felt somewhere deep inside me that it was time. So I surrendered control; I indulged the hunger of my body, and it filled and swelled, smothering my lovely hipbones, until it attained this grotesque shape of the third boob, which makes professionalism quite impossible, because professionalism equals control equals denial of hunger equals a woman's body stripped of its breasts and hips and belly and period and pared down to look as hard and streamlined and non-threatening as a man's body (as long as they smile benignly and pretend not to have penises).

At Andover from 1975 to 1977, I studied Virgil in the original Latin, read the major documents of American history in the original sources, won an English prize for an essay on *Hamlet,* took a course in the biology of cancer, and lived with my entire urban studies class in a Boston brownstone while I did an internship at the *Boston Globe.* I also learned to drink, to get stoned, to dump a boy before he could dump me, and to wear boys' clothing. This last was an expensive lesson, as my mother had taken me out shopping just before school started, outfitting me with a complete wardrobe of high-waisted, elephant-leg, bell-bottom blue jeans, floral blouses, shoes with fashionable clunky heels, and a new pocketbook. I understood that it wasn't just money my mother was spending on me, but love; I had heard often enough her stories of being young and poor and shabby, of how her parents had not considered her good appearance a valid expense.

But then I got up to school and noted immediately The Look. The ideal Andover girl, of whom there were actually an intimidating number, dressed in boys' straight-leg Levis; boys' button-down Oxford shirts, with the tails hanging out; boys' cable-knit wool fishermen's sweaters, oversized; and big rugged hiking boots. She had medium-length brownish-blond hair that was not in any way fussed with, nor did she wear makeup, but her face was naturally beautiful, with high cheekbones, a small, tasteful nose, perfect skin, and blue eyes that were never soft and inviting, but rather cold and tough; and she rarely smiled. And, of course, she had a body that looked good in those clothes: minimal breasts, flat belly, long, lanky legs. It was a miracle of gender transubstantiation, this elite New England WASP sexual aesthetic: The more boyish she looked, the more "feminine" she was. *Write on the blackboard a thousand times: I will look like a boy, act like a boy, perform like a boy. And more of a man each day.* My second day in Andover, I went shopping for a new wardrobe that cost me half my first year's allowance, and hid the unworn clothes my mother had bought me at the bottom of my trunk.

That fall I was very homesick and often lingered on the streets of Andover at dusk, watching the lights come on in the big Victorian houses, dawdling to stare at the jack-o'-lanterns on the front porches and the childish crayon drawings in the windows, sniffing like a pauper at the aromas of pot roast and apple crisp and woodsmoke that drifted outward on the frosty air and mixed with the rich scent of rotting leaves. There was something in those houses that I longed for desperately, but I sensed that it was too late for me now to get it back; it had outlived its usefulness for my survival. For this was about the time, I realize in retrospect, that my childhood ended, and my résumé began.

THE ABYSS

CHICAGO—Desperately, I find myself suggesting to the interviewer that the paper must have night and weekend shifts, which are unpopular with most people but would be perfect for me. I am imagining that I will care for the baby while Ellis is at work, and run out the door to a job of my own the moment he returns. Afterward, I am ashamed of myself; how I care for this baby is none of the interviewer's business. However, I am forced for the first time to recognize that I simply have not thought this question through. I have somehow assumed that feminists have worked this kind of thing out by now, as though they had discovered a cure for cancer. I know there is a solution known as Day Care, but it is not until this exact moment of being fully irrevocably imminently on the verge of giving birth that I have thought to face the reality: *What* day care? There is no money for a nanny. There is no willing aunt or grandmother in the wings. Ellis has not expressed any desire to become a homemaker, nor can we, at the moment, afford for him to work less than full-time, since any entry-level journalism job I get would pay less than half of what he already earns, and we can barely afford the rent on our run-down Chicago apartment.

But there is something else: I *want* to mother this baby—at least more than simply on evenings and weekends. And once I acknowledge this, I see a huge and terrifying abyss open up beneath my feet. I don't know how to see myself as female, without taunting myself with derogatory connotations; I don't know how to choose to do something "feminine" without immediately discounting it as worthless, a nonachievement. All those years spent trying to be a boy, trying so desperately to minimize the significance of having a female body; all those years spent identifying myself as a feminist, thinking that what that *meant* was trying to minimize the significance of having a female body; all those years of fierce insistence that this body must never be allowed to define Me. And though I am still sure that it doesn't, completely, here is my belly going before me like a megaphone, screaming something else to the world, the world of men—the only world whose standards I have ever used to measure myself—commanding it to draw its own conclusions.

It astounds me, in retrospect, how intimate we all became immediately. Within a month we were having big communal dinners at one another's apartments, with enormous vegetable lasagnas and salads and jugs of red wine. We were excited by the way the husbands seemed to hit it off, since they complained to us all the time that they felt so isolated in their roles as fathers. When we first saw them together in Grace's living room, balancing their beers on one knee and their toddlers on the other, and arguing happily over what famous person had said "There is no distinctly native American criminal class except Congress" rather than the merits of the Cubs, the Bulls, or the Bears, it was clear that they shared the same sense of humor and sensibility. We began encouraging them to go out together for drinks or movies, imagining that they would form some sort of Playgroup Male Auxiliary and work through their fatherhood ambivalences in conversation.

Actually, it was Angie who was the conductor of all this intimacy. Grace and I still couldn't quite get beyond arm's length. Now that I knew her a little better, I began to interpret her reticence as an extreme form of politeness designed to disguise her disapproval of practically everything I did: my thoughtless meat- and sugar-eating habits; my letting Sam watch Disney videos and Saturday morning cartoons; my entrusting Sam two-and-a-half days a week to outside day care. And when Phoebe picked up Sam's Proton Pak or his plastic medieval sword and helmet, Grace's voice always got a little higher and a little more musical with the strain of trying to remain open-minded.

Much later, however, Grace told me she always assumed I disapproved of *her*, and that was part of the reason for her reticence. But in the meantime Angie spanned the distance between us, which was easy for her in part because she was such a chameleon. With Grace she ordered Japanese seaweed crackers in bulk from a health food wholesaler; for me she brought out the squares of Swiss chocolate she had hidden in the back of the refrigerator. She quizzed Grace constantly about homeopathic remedies and child-led weaning, and me about antibiotics and finding good child care, as though in one or the other set of values she would find the code that would finally make sense of her life—the pattern in the quilt. The way she nibbled at us reminded me of a roommate I had in college, who tended to become obsessed with certain people because, she said, she would suddenly be overwhelmed by the feeling that she needed a piece of their soul for herself. I remember being fascinated by the remark, because obviously it was a little unbalanced, but on the other hand it so perfectly expressed the essence of why anyone becomes friends with anybody, or falls in love.

The thing about Angie was that she never took without giving back. You confided in her because at the surface she had that chameleon's quality of reflecting back at you what you appeared (or tried to make yourself appear) to be; and then, underneath her facade of hip, cynical cheerfulness, you sensed a well of sadness so deep and dark that no confidence poured into it could ever reflect a harsh light back at you. She was generous with what she referred to as "treats," small winning gifts or acts of empathy: a pair of funky, colorful earrings when I was pregnant the second time, and just beginning to waddle; a paper bag of lollipops left lying in the vestibule when Sam had strep throat and the two of us could not come out to play; and early on, after that first playgroup conversation about childbirth, a book by the artist Judy Chicago, called *The Birth Project*.

The book chronicles a vast exhibit of birth images conceived by Chicago and executed in needlework over the course of five years by women volunteers in homes across the United States, Canada, and New Zealand. They are extraordinarily striking images, richly colored and textured, with strong, explosive lines: forms of women radiating heat and power, their breasts and hips like mountains, splitting open with a birth force that runs through them like molten lava. Collectively they manage to convey all the great conflicting elements of birth—its pain, its mystery, its terror, its violence, and its magnificence. They are graphic and thoroughly honest images, so rooted in the processes of the body that they cannot be said to be in very good taste. And yet I found them beautiful. They reflected exactly what I had felt myself and told the playgroup, about standing alone before the great god, or goddess.

◈

"So," said Angie, setting down two decaffeinated cappuccinos on one of the rickety tabletops at the Café Espresso. "Do you think our two votes are going to make the crucial difference?"

We had spent the cold, early November afternoon pushing our strollers from church basement to school lobby to church basement, trying to find our correct respective polling places, which turned out to be different despite the fact that we lived within two blocks of one another. Miraculously, Sam and Gabriel had finally both fallen asleep, allowing us to stop at the trendy café on Main Street. The Café Espresso posted the geographical and political pedigrees of its coffee beans, and was always full of people reading, writing, or trying to look as though they were reading or writing. Because of its two walls of windows overlooking a busy intersection, it happened to be one of the few restaurants that didn't make me faint with claustrophobia.

"I'm sure mine doomed Dukakis," I said. "My approval is always a sign that a candidate is going to lose big."

"I know exactly what you mean. But I can't figure out why that is. Like, do you personally know anyone who would vote for Bush?"

"Actually, I think my father probably will. But then my mother will vote Democratic and cancel him out."

I smiled at my old family joke, but Angie said, "Or maybe your mom votes Democratic and your dad cancels her out. Doesn't it make you feel totally powerless? I mean, why bother?"

I tried to think of a good reason. "I guess," I said finally, "because it's the absolute least you can do. Really, we should be going to NOW meetings every month and showing up at clinics to protest those Operation Rescue people."

"You know what, though, Nina?" Angie said slowly. "I think those NOW people are kind of fucked up. And even though I had an abortion myself, in college?" Her voice rose questioningly, and she paused here for my affirmative nod before she went on. "I think now that I've actually had a kid I would find it hard to march around with a sign promoting it."

"But they're not *promoting* it," I said. "They're just trying to protect the right of women who are in situations like you must have been in to exercise that choice."

"But you know what I mean?" Angie persisted. "Now that you went through pregnancy and looked at all those week-by-week pictures of growing fetuses and imagined it happening inside you and saw this really amazing, helpless thing that came out at the end, and nursed it and smelled the way it

smells, doesn't it make you feel kind of—" Angie struggled for
a moment to think of the proper word. "—kind of *oogy* just to
think about?"

We both looked for a moment at our sons, slumped awkwardly in their strollers. Gabriel's arm was locked around a
woolly thing he almost never let go of that had once been a
sheep or a bunny or a bear but was now eroded beyond identi-
fication. His face was angelic, wiped clean of the willfulness
and mischievousness that Angie was always complaining
about.

Sam was snoring softly, his face crunched into a slight
frown. Not even sleep seemed to relax his mind or ease the
pangs of his need. As an infant, in sleep his small mouth
would work and suck as he dreamed of nursing. But it was
never a blissful dreaming. Always he wore that frown, as
though something were slightly amiss, some sustenance sought
that could not be found.

"Yes," I said. "It definitely makes me feel, um, oogier than it
used to make me feel. I definitely feel now that it would be
killing something. I don't think it's something I could possibly
do right now. But I still don't think that's the point."

We sipped cappuccino for a moment in silence. Then I said,
"Why do you think the NOW people are fucked up?"

"Well, aren't they the ones who were telling us all those
years that we should be just like men? Like that stuff you were
saying at playgroup one day about women controlling their
destinies and acting just like guys, and how after you have a
baby you find out you can't really live like that?"

"But I keep thinking we *could* really live like that if we
could ever get men to take their families as seriously as women
are willing to take their careers."

"Well," said Angie, "I know I didn't take *my* career very seriously. And I know that's some kind of major feminist sin.
But there's no way I can tell myself that going into some of-

fice building five days a week, fifty weeks of every year, to think up computer programs just so the executives and stockholders of this company can make lots and lots of money is as important as the fact that I made another human being inside my body and now I'm trying to raise him.

"But I've been reading this book *Men and Marriage* by this guy George Gilder, have you ever heard of him?" Angie went on.

"Yeah," I said. "He's a fairly famous male chauvinist."

"Are you sure?" asked Angie, suspiciously. "Because what he actually says in this book is that women really *are* the superior sex, and that men are total pigs and savages. He says men have this big natural urge to go off by themselves and build things and have wars, and that if women didn't have this big natural urge to keep on making babies and domesticate men and keep them from killing each other off completely, there would be no civilization."

I laughed. "Well, there's probably some truth to that. But I have a big natural urge to go off by myself, too. Not to have a war, but definitely to build things. I mean, I *do* have a strong domestic instinct, but I also have a really strong counter-domestic instinct. I have this fantasy, sometimes, of what my life would be like if I hadn't gotten married and had kids, and I can see myself in New York in an apartment by myself, smoking cigarettes and writing books and being really happy.

"And besides," I said, "don't you think there's something really patronizing about a *man* calling women the 'superior' sex? Usually men do that to justify confining women to domestic roles, so they can hoard all the political power for themselves."

"All I know," said Angie, "is that it seems to be true in my marriage. I wanted Jeff to be just like me about parenting, and he's not. He's gone twelve hours a day to do this job that he says is incredibly important, that his company says is very important, that business leaders and politicians and even *feminists* say is really important, and I'm at home doing this thing that no one except George Gilder and *Mothering* magazine says is important."

There was a long, uncomfortable silence. Suddenly I thought of the Judy Chicago book.

"Do you remember what she said in the Introduction and the Afterword to *The Birth Project?*" I asked.

"Actually, I'm not sure I ever read it," Angie said. "I was mostly just interested in the images."

So I told Angie the story Judy Chicago tells in the Introduction—the story behind the project, and behind her decision as an artist to work with textiles. She describes her early training in the very male field of classical art, and her struggle for acceptance as "one of the boys." At first, she carefully observed the distinction between "art" and "craft," knowing that there were certain media in which one could not work and be taken seriously as an artist. But she had explored many other nontraditional techniques, including fireworks and spraypainting, which she had learned in largely male workplaces, including auto body school, where the men had harassed her. During the seventies, she writes, she began to understand that she could not forever deny her femaleness.

So she began to study women's history, and to think about the fact that the fundamental difference between men and women is that women give birth. But when she went to research images of birth, she was "struck dumb" when her research turned up none. "It was obvious that birth was a universal human experience and one that is central to women's lives," she writes. "Attracted to the void, I plunged into the subject."

The result was this series of images, which she decided to execute in needlework because it seemed appropriate to use a "female" medium for a female subject. Because the scale of the project was so vast, she needed a large pool of volunteer needleworkers; and, too, a participatory approach seemed appropriate because traditionally women have performed needlework in groups.

Judy Chicago made a clear association between two forms of female creativity—birth and needlework—and obviously hoped to use the exhibition to insist that both be taken seriously. But the book's Afterword is full of her ambivalence and bitterness about the project. She was extremely frustrated by the "lack of professionalism" among her volunteer stitchers, which she saw as distinctly feminine: their inability to understand the power politics of the art world and their failure to match her artistic commitment (she gripes that the women, many of whom presumably had family responsibilities, might only spend eight to ten hours a week on the work, while she herself spent eight to ten hours a day).

And in the end, she did not manage to single-handedly raise the consciousness of the art world. She was snubbed by museums and galleries all across the country. She notes that it drove her "wild with frustration" that the many women in expensive cars who drove out to her gallery to see the work "were frequently moved to tears by what we were doing but left without writing a check." She ends the book, sounding utterly disillusioned, saying she plans henceforth to retreat to her studio to create in privacy.

"So what's your point?" Angie asked, when I had told her the whole story.

"My point is that Judy Chicago got trapped in the jaws of the paradox she was trying to expose. As long as she did male subjects in male ways, she was successful. But the moment she tried to say, 'Wait a minute, take *this* seriously,' and she said it in a female way, the art world sat down on her. And that's the condition of women in America today: As long as they go along and follow the path the feminists blazed, of doing the things men think are important and doing them the way men do, they'll get approval. But you're right, having kids is not one of those things. People give it lip service, but when you actually commit yourself to it, everyone sits down on you."

Sam had opened his eyes and was looking dazedly around the café. He was disoriented, and I could tell he was about to cry, so I began to talk fast.

"But see, Angie, that was always true. Before feminism, women were still trapped and sat on, only they didn't have any voice to talk back."

"MAMA!" went Sam, emerging from sleep in panic, as he always seemed to do.

His yell woke Gabriel, who also looked cranky. People began to turn toward our table in irritation. Angie and I got up hastily and pulled on our jackets.

Out on the street, our breath came out in big white clouds.

"Are Jeff and Ellis still going out tonight?" asked Angie.

"As far as I know," I said. "I think they're going to see *Friday the Thirteenth, Part Twenty-Seven.*"

"Oh, yeah? Does Ellis really get into that kind of stuff? He seems like he'd be real intellectual, like you could take him to a French movie and he wouldn't make fun of it."

"No, he'd make fun of it," I said, and turned my stroller toward home. It was too cold on the corner to stand and chat, and besides, there was something about the tone in Angie's voice when she asked me questions about Ellis that always made me uncomfortable.

CHAPTER 3

MARRIAGE STORY

ANGIE

[A] novel, the sort of novel one could imagine one's life to
be, at any rate, appears to meander, with a ragbag of concerns. . . . You try to direct your life along the route of beginning, middle, and end, but actually life has a sprinkling of
beginnings and middles and ends all the way through, not in
the right order.

Lynn Sharon Schwartz, Disturbances in the Field

■ ■ ■

She could not find a story that fit her. She had gone through
life leaping boldly and hopefully from one identity to the
next, foreseeing in each new person or new opportunity the
One True Defining Answer that would make her feel whole
and sufficient, rather than fragmented and defective. Good
Girl, Bad Girl, Daughter, Orphan, Student, Girlfriend, Lover,
Wife, Earth Mother—any one of these identities could have
defined a whole life for another woman. Or collectively they
might have been stitched together, nine neat schematic
squares in a decorative or symbolic pattern, forming something coherent and recognizably a Life.

Only they weren't neat, and they couldn't be stitched together, because there wasn't any pattern to them that Angie
could detect. They were a mismatched scrap heap of
dropped and aborted undertakings, and looking them over
tended to make an emotion mixed of shame and panic rise in
her throat, so she very rarely did, but rather kept the whole
mess shoved away in a drawer in her mind, thinking someday

she might get back to it and clean it up, if she ever had any energy.

Meanwhile, in her imagination was the vision of the quilt that could be made without squares, that would express something bolder and more honestly lifelike. If only she could discover the appropriate technique, and not be interrupted by her own self-doubt. Thus, for validation, she was drawn to other people who seemed to be living slightly outside the squares themselves, and recognized it.

That was what she had seen in Grace, who at first glance seemed to have stepped out of the pages of *Mothering* magazine, where the child was the center of the universe and the parents were like adoring, orbiting satellites shining down warmth and spirituality and nurturance twenty-four hours a day. This was in the phase when Angie had thought *Mothering* (as well as Mothering itself) was The Answer, but was discovering that few of the actual suggestions, such as having the baby sleep in your bed and not vaccinating him against childhood illnesses and having him run around outside in a little pair of soft moccasins so as not to distort the shape of his feet, worked for her. After a while, you started to feel that the people who really fit into those supposedly Alternative squares were just as conventional as the regular people, if not more so, because to really pull all that stuff off you couldn't have any life or needs or desires of your own, you were just the slave of your child and you were supposed to love it.

But Grace was obviously ambivalent about it. She had given up a career as a theater director, not because she planned to, but because she discovered you couldn't nurse a baby on demand—at least not a demanding baby—and also direct plays. Angie spent a lot of time and energy trying to determine exactly what it cost Grace to let that go, especially given Grace's endless patience with Phoebe. Phoebe was the kind of baby who never wanted to let Grace out of her sight and screamed if she tried to leave and grabbed toys away from Gabriel (who was only about half her size), in a way that seemed purely mean, like she didn't really want the toy but was just picking on him because she knew he would get upset. Angie sometimes felt herself fill with irrational anger, watching Phoebe, and thought if it were *her* kid, it would be hard sometimes not to just smack her. And eventually Grace's endless patience, which had seemed so admirable, began to strike Angie as irritating, and to get in the way of the friendship.

Plus Grace's marriage was kind of irritating. Her husband Michael was totally committed as a father. He worked on his dissertation in the basement of their building and came home for lunch, was home for the evening by five, liked to shop for and cook their organic vegetarian dinners, and sometimes came up during the day and took Phoebe if Grace had an appointment somewhere. So, of course, with a husband like that giving you some support for what you were doing, you might have the energy to put up with more shit.

Then Nina came along, like something out of the mainstream magazines, and it immediately seemed like she might have The Answer. (The opposite Answer.) Those are the magazines where the Mommy and the Daddy are very brisk, busy people with lots of important things to do and they have a microwave and a minivan and a baby and when they aren't using the minivan they park it in the garage and when they aren't using the baby they park it with the nanny. Only obviously Nina didn't quite fit into that little square either. She was driven, but she worked only two-and-a-half days a week because, she said, that was the maximum amount of time she felt she could tolerate day care and the minimum amount of time that could keep her writing self alive.

Angie was fascinated by Nina's marriage. Ellis was not a Mr. Supportive type who willingly diapered and cooked. He had reacted to fatherhood in the same way as her own husband, Jeff: He seemed to want to avoid it as much as possible. He reminded her a lot of Jeff, actually, which was maybe why the four of them got along so well. He had the same quick-witted, verbal sense of humor that camouflaged something he didn't want you to know about him, either that he was Very Nice (which can be a very sexy quality in a man) or that he was Very Not-Nice (which can also be a very sexy quality). They were different physically, though; whereas Jeff was tall and blond and thin to the point almost of fragility, Ellis was of medium height, with a strong, powerful build, and dark haired, with a handsome, angular face. When he was around, Angie felt physically uncomfortable, overwhelmed and a little short of breath, but it was exciting to flirt with him; it reminded her of what her relationship had once been like with Jeff, and of that glorious giddy sense she had had long ago, that there might be a *man* who would be The Answer.

◆

The only reason they got married in the first place was that they had agreed about rewriting the old marriage story. In 1983 people just did not get married as blindly as they once had—expecting the wife to obey the husband, expecting the husband to support the wife financially, or even expecting that marriage was the kind of commitment that lasts a lifetime.

Getting married in 1983 was almost a tongue-in-cheek kind of thing to do. It was a mostly androgynous act that declared to the world that you were Best Buddies going off on an adventure together, but you'd probably already been sleeping together for years and you were really just formalizing things, making it okay for your mom and dad to admit you were sleeping together, making it a little easier to spend

Christmas and Thanksgiving as a couple, eliminating that awkward little problem of how to refer to the other person (although the terms *husband* and *wife* seemed so hopelessly middle-aged and retro).

They met in college, in 1979, at the beginning of her junior year. She worked shifts with him in a dorm sundries shop, where they sold Chee-tos to the other students and pilfered from the stock themselves. It seemed important that he could steal as well as she could; it set a certain outlaw tone, the us-against-them glue that is so important early in a relationship: the miracle of being loved for those parts of yourself that you have always assumed are responsible for your sense of exile from the rest of the human race. She loved everything that was wrong with him: that he was so thin and pale he appeared breakable; that he either talked too little (he was shy) or too much (once he got started, it was hard to stop him); that he was too smart and studied too hard (she went to the library at night and tried to lure him out, then did everything she could, including cheating, to beat him out on tests in classes they took together); that he was sexually adventurous (there was something exploratory in high school, with another boy). And he must have loved all those things that were wrong with her: her academic delinquency (he said she'd be brilliant if only she applied herself, and he turned her on to programming); the way she was damaged sexually ("I know I have to think of something to keep you interested," he teased as he tugged her pants down, " 'cuz at any minute you might run up that old white flag"); and the sheer intensity of her need. But no, it was probably not so much that he loved her need as that she had finally succeeded in subduing it, covering it up, smothering it under a cool, flippant demeanor. That was the point, after all, of stealing: to be able to get the things you need without having to seek other people's permission or their cooperation. And that wasn't the kind of lesson you were born knowing; it was the kind of wisdom you acquired with experience.

◆

Quilt square: Girlfriend—Other girls got crushes, but Angie fell in love. Constantly. From the time she got her period in fifth grade, she was in and out of love every couple of weeks. Over and over, this rising, euphoric wave of conviction that *this* guy was really It, and then the break of the wave as it crashed into reality, because, of course, how many twelve- or thirteen-year-old boys can deliver the substance of being It?

Until she met Rafe, right before she started high school. He lived just around the block, and owned a motorcycle, and he *looked* like a guy with a motorcycle: black leather jacket, greasy hair, tight blue jeans, sullen face. An outlaw, for sure. Angie thought he was gorgeous, and within weeks she began to look like a girl who went with a guy who had a motorcycle. In photos from that period, she slouches and her hair hangs in her face and you cannot see what is in her eyes.

In the crawl space beneath Rafe's porch, where they kissed and touched each other's bodies, Angie drifted off into a hazy, dreamlike state. Once she thought afterward that he might have penetrated her, because she hurt Down There and when she peed she felt raw, but she wasn't exactly sure because when it happened she hadn't been there with him, she'd been off in the safe, dreamy place by herself, where the things her parents told her were so Bad turned out actually to be so very Good.

But then her parents caught on. She wasn't studying, wasn't even pretending to study, and one day she came home with an F. Plus, Rafe was a motorcycle guy, he had important things to take care of, he couldn't just hang around making out all the time. He'd be nasty to Angie on the phone, and she'd burst into tears. But then she'd go sit out on the front porch for hours, just in case he passed by.

Her parents told her they weren't going to let her ruin her life for some good-for-nothing juvenile delinquent, and they sent her away for three weeks to cousins in Wisconsin. When she came home, she heard that Rafe was having awful headaches and wouldn't come out of his house, but that was okay. Because Angie had recognized how much nicer and safer life could be in the kind of tiny little farm town where everyone knew everyone else and sat out on lawn chairs in the front yard every evening talking about the weather and gazing up at the stars.

Angie and Jeff agreed on the two basic components of a revisionist marriage: You didn't want stereotypical sex-role behavior, and you didn't want kids. And these things were just a given, because by the time they got married they'd been living in each other's dorm rooms and wearing each other's clothes and getting identical haircuts for years, and Angie, who was two years ahead of Jeff in school, had already been working as a programmer for a while. And they had both felt very strongly since long before they met that they would never, ever want to have kids.

Their idea—the story they had agreed upon, if you will— was that you both got jobs that paid you decently enough to live, and you lived your Real Life outside the jobs: in the conversations you had at home, the movies you saw, the food you ate, the spirituality you cultivated in yourself. And you did all of this consciously, and this was the point of life itself, this journey that involved eating for your own health and for the planet's, dressing from thrift shops to avoid the crass commercial culture, and, in Angie's case, designing and sewing your own clothes, to combine artistic self-expression with pragmatism. They both agreed that Jeff would make a great teacher, and that this would be in a sense his own personal ministry, his way of doing good among the young, since they were not going to reproduce themselves.

And that was why Angie believed that Jeff was the first to betray the pact. Because, right out of school, he signed up with BDCC, the Big Damn Computer Company, a multinational giant teeming with Ivy Leaguers in expensive clothes jogging relentlessly around the Management Track, with smiles on their faces and their elbows pointing viciously out. She simply could not believe the serious expression on Jeff's face as he explained to her that, while the entry-level salaries were not big, relative to other companies, the opportunities for advancement were unsurpassed. BDCC offered the best people to work with, the most interesting projects, terrific benefits, world travel, and, of course, the paycheck would grow as he reached management level.

Now, where Jeff came from, security meant hanging on to your job at the gas pump for dear life. He had grown up in some tiny little town in Kentucky where the men shot up each other's pickup trucks for fun and the little boys walked around in bib overalls with one strap hanging down and the girls bore babies at such a tender age there was no such thing as a generation gap. His model for true success and affluence was Darren on *Bewitched*, and you could see that being treated as an equal by these Ivy League types was like walking into fairyland for him, something he never imagined could take place in his actual Real Life. And it was suddenly more real to him than the thrift shop clothes and cultivating the spiritual side of himself. His idea of spirituality, now, was one of those weekends where they dragged his whole department to the "campus" way west of Chicago and made them play Outward Bound games to encourage interpersonal bonding.

Angie *hated* BDCC. She couldn't say exactly why she felt so strongly—somehow it seemed obvious that any reasonable person would—but when she tried to explain it to someone, she could always see they didn't quite *get* it. It was almost like watching your husband have an affair—get swept up in some passion you just couldn't share, that suddenly became the essence of his existence and excluded you. Lots of people apparently considered that to be a normal way of life, and went on that way for years, but she and Jeff weren't normal and that was why they were together. And dammit, they had an agreement.

So after about a year, she got him to quit. He didn't want to. When she reminded him about the teaching, he said they couldn't afford for him to go back and get his teaching certificate if it would mean living off the $22,000 she made at her job. "If I could get twenty-six or twenty-eight at another company," Angie asked, "would you do it?"

Jeff gasped and said she couldn't possibly get that much. (He made only $22,000 himself.)

She knew it was almost impossible to get him untangled from something once he thought he'd made a commitment. So the day she got a job offer for $28,000, she stopped at a travel agency and bought two plane tickets.

"Three weeks," she told Jeff. "France, England, Italy, Germany."

"They'll *never* give me three weeks off. If you ask for more than two, that's like saying you're not putting the company first."

"Hmmm. Maybe this would be a good time to quit. I mean, do you want to put the company first? Or do you want to see France, England, Italy, and Germany?"

Jeff thought about it overnight. He was not, after all,

pumping gas like his forefathers in Homer Creek. The next day he went in to work and quit, and came home with two huge backpacks.

◈

Quilt square: Bad Girl—Angie discovered stealing in junior high. She'd be out with a group of friends from school, and they'd dare one another to see who could get the best stuff. Clothes, jewelry, accessories. Angie quickly realized not only that she was better at it than everyone else, but that she liked doing it more. Because it didn't seem *fair* that she couldn't get all that stuff that she needed, until she discovered that she *could* get it. She had always been such a good girl, and it had never gotten her anywhere, although now she could see that all those techniques of good-girlness were turning out to be useful. She was quick with her hands and clever about where she hid the stuff, but what really fooled them every time was the way she looked them straight in the eye, her face full of sweet innocence.

Her parents, of course, eventually caught on, and started asking a lot of questions, and making her bring home receipts. But that was simply another challenge. She liked coming up with the stories to fool them with. She kept going out stealing after school. She was out stealing, in fact, the day the ambulance and the police cars raced up to the little working-class suburban bungalow and took her mother away.

"She took pills," said Angie's grandmother, who was making dinner in the kitchen. "Your father couldn't wake her up. He went with her to the hospital."

"She's going to be all right," her father said late that night, when all four children had gathered around the dining room table. "But she can't cope with being home right now, so the doctors say she'll have to stay in the hospital and rest."

He went on to explain that the doctors felt it was very important for them all to talk about their feelings right now. Not to outsiders, who might not understand, who might judge them, but to one another, or, if they wished, to a therapist.

Angie told her best friend, but no one else. She wasn't interested in talking to a therapist. She went right on stealing until her mother got home from the hospital and started demanding receipts again, and for a while Angie distracted her by providing them, but then her mother went searching through her room and found a stash of items for which there were no receipts.

Then Angie was made to write a list of everything she had stolen and how much it had cost, and to get a part-time job, and to go from store to store with little white envelopes full of money, until she had paid them all back.

◈

For a while after they got back from Europe, it seemed they had attained the perfect eighties marriage. Every day, Angie went off to her programming job with a lunch packed by Jeff. He cleaned and shopped and cooked and went to class two days a week to get his teaching certificate. In his free time, he was reading his way through the spiritual history of humanity.

Jeff had had no formal religious training, and referred to his family affiliation as "White Trash Protestant." When he was going out with the girlfriend before Angie, who was Jewish, he had hung out a lot with her brother, who had lived on a kibbutz in Israel and kept kosher, and Jeff had enrolled himself in a Hebrew class, studied the Torah, and considered himself a conservative Jew for about a year.

After Angie came along, he asked her to take him to Mass,

and decided that Catholicism was a logical spiritual leap from Judaism, toward a closer relationship with God. And by now he was reading the Catholic mystics, who were truly intimate with Him—none of this prayer stuff, where you put it in the mail to Him and hope He sends back an answer someday, but real conversations directly with Him. He saw an analogy to computer programming, which was ostensibly about all kinds of rules and order but was actually, for those who were truly gifted, a deeply intuitive process.

He was deep in the writings of Dorothy Day, the layperson who founded the Catholic Worker movement to bring the doctrine of charity to life by feeding, clothing, and respecting the poor and homeless in the heart of America's cities. Dorothy Day had believed it was still possible in our own time to live as Jesus had lived; and Jeff, who had just seen the light and cast off his greedy, Yuppie ways, was inspired.

So here was The Answer: They would give away—not even sell, but *give away*—all of their material possessions. And they would go live in Ann Arbor, a town where they had heard people still honored sixties values, and they could live cheaply while they contacted the Peace Corps and the Catholic Worker people and the handful of private schools Jeff would apply to, which didn't require a state certification. Angie's parents couldn't stand it, watching those bikes and pots and pans and wedding presents go out the door; they kept coming over to pack up boxes to store in their attic, because "you're going to want this later."

They arrived in Ann Arbor on the bus with one trunk, their backpacks, and Angie's sewing machine, on a beautiful spring day in 1985. At first it was all perfect. They went to Mass every morning. They worked twice a week at the co-op grocery and bakery to get their food, and helped the landlord with odd jobs in exchange for rent reductions. With a few thousand dollars in savings, they could still afford movies and cheap dinners out.

Jeff worked three days a week at a homeless shelter, where he told himself: Everyone you meet is Christ, or could be. He didn't literally believe that, of course, but it helped break down the barriers. The men who came in drunk, reeking of alcohol and vomit, the psychotics who came in ranting about their own encounters with God and the Devil—they scared him at first. But he made himself talk to them, treat them respectfully, open himself to them, and after a while be began to feel—just as he had felt with the Ivy Leaguers who intimidated him at BDCC—the underlying kinship that meant they were all essentially alike. This knowledge seemed to him liberating and exhilarating, for if a person could move with ease from Homer Creek to BDCC to skid row, then there was nowhere to rise to and nowhere to fall from, and spiritually, one was always safe.

But on Angie, the homeless shelter had the opposite effect. The sight of those ragged, battered, unwanted men knocked loose some cork within her, flooding her with terror and panic. The seat of her emotions was some kind of black hole that sucked in other people's pain and need and despair and made it all her own. And these lost men embodied something she didn't want to see and couldn't tolerate, a thing she had always known about herself but could never, ever voice.

Before they'd had a chance to make up their minds about the Catholic Worker business, word came from a Catholic boys' school near Chicago that they wanted to hire Jeff.

"Let's go," Angie said immediately. "I know you'll make a great teacher."

And Jeff, now serene and confident, agreed.

Quilt square: Orphan—She was five years old. She and her friends were playing in the dark hall closet with one of those toy slide projectors that shine cartoon images on the wall. Angie came out of the closet and found her mother leaning against the wall, crying—huge gulping sobs of hopelessness that went on and on. Angie tried to stop her, she felt she would do anything to stop her, but when she asked if there was anything she could do, her mother just shook her head no, and slowly slid down against the wall until she was sitting on the hall floor, moaning. A while after that, her mother disappeared, for weeks, or was it months? Her father said some doctors were going to help her feel better, and then she would come home.

◆

Angie took to buying *Mothering* magazine at the organic food store where they shopped. The thing that Jeff seemed to find in religion—the comfort of the rules and regulations after the chaos of his childhood, the balm of the soothing doctrine on a wound he didn't know he still felt—was what Angie found in its pages. She was mesmerized by its images of plain-looking, bare-breasted women nursing toddlers; of women hiking up mountain trails with babies in backpacks; of naked, spread-legged women delivering babies in their beds at home, their faces contorted in orgasmic pleasure-pain, their husbands holding one leg while the midwife held the other.

"You don't *ever* want to have a kid?" she asked Jeff one night, as they lay on their futon on the floor of the darkened studio apartment.

Jeff groaned. "Angie, come on. They're insatiable. They're squalling, whining brats who eat their parents up." Jeff's half brother and half sister were a decade younger than he was, and he claimed to be able to remember this quite vividly.

Angie propped herself up on one elbow. "You just *think* it has to be like that because of the way our parents were. They *let* themselves get eaten up. But we wouldn't be like that."

"How would we be?"

"We would treat the baby with respect. We would take it with us places, really include it in our lives. It wouldn't be like the Grown-ups against the Kids, it would be like we were all equals."

Jeff was quiet.

"Like, I wouldn't want it to call me Mommy. I would want it to call me by my name."

"I think we should wait a while, anyway," Jeff said, finally. "When we met, you were totally against having kids. I just can't believe it's something we should do impulsively."

"Well, yeah," said Angie. "Of course. Only, I don't think we should keep our minds totally closed to it."

They drifted off to sleep, secure in the warmth and oneness of their bodies pressed close under the quilt. He was thinking: "I hope she gives up." And she was thinking: "I bet he gives in."

Meanwhile, the thing Angie had seen in the homeless shelter in Ann Arbor, Jeff found in a Catholic school full of upper-middle-class white teenage boys. He had imagined something like *Room 222*, him sitting around rapping, dispensing not just book-learning, but wisdom about Life Itself. He had been such a motivated, genuinely *interested* student himself that he could picture his charges only as empty vessels waiting to be filled.

They ate him for lunch. They were adolescent boys; they spotted his weaknesses like cavities and drilled into them relentlessly. They mocked him and defied him, and he felt so personally *hurt* that he could not summon up the authority to impose order on them. His inner self, which only a few months before had been as spiritually unassailable as a Venetian fortress, had turned to tender flesh, and was being battered raw.

He came home each night in tears. "Just quit," Angie told him, but he had this funny thing about seeing his commitments through to the bitter end, and wouldn't hear of it. His leg went inexplicably numb, and there were days he couldn't physically drag himself out of bed. As winter came on, he began to hallucinate; little voices jumped unbidden into his mind.

"QUIT!" said Angie. "Don't you see, you're killing yourself for these brats."

And finally, because he felt the absolute impossibility of returning after Christmas break, he did. Angie had never seen him fail at anything, and it scared her, watching him go through it. But once he was out and started to relax, she started to relax, too, and she couldn't help thinking that after his arrogance at BDCC and his righteousness at the homeless shelter, he'd probably needed something like this to cool his jets. And she liked his newly humbled self.

◆

Quilt square: Good Girl—In second grade, she was such a good little student that once a teacher from the eighth grade came down and asked her up to the eighth-grade classroom. Then, in front of the class, the teacher started asking her all kinds of geography questions that the eighth graders had not been able to answer, and Angie answered them correctly, one after another. She was aware every moment of how important it was to please the teacher, and also of how humiliated the eighth graders were being made to feel, and how much they must hate her. But many years later, she was still mystified by how she had gone from being such a bright little girl to being what the teachers in high school told her parents and her parents told her was called an "underachiever."

◈

Jeff found a new programming job with a mail-order house in the western suburbs, an undemanding job where he could put in his eight hours and leave, and dress in thrift-shop clothing. Angie worked at the Westerville library circulation desk and spent lots of time quilting and designing loose, funky, colorful outfits for herself. They fell in with a crowd of hip singles who lived on their block, and took turns cooking big vegetarian dinners and Sunday brunches where everybody lay around talking and reading the paper and whoever got up first had to make the next pot of coffee.

As relentlessly as a drumbeat coming closer in the forest, the nighttime conversations continued.

"Our mothers just got stuck with it," Angie would begin. "I'm saying, I really want to do it as my career."

"It's not a career, Angie. It's a job, a blue-collar job, like mixing cement or something. It's changing diapers and wiping up puke and putting Band-Aids on. It's mostly shitwork."

"How can you say that? You didn't think working in the homeless shelter was shitwork, and that was all about shit and puke."

"That was about helping to clean up some of the shit that already exists in the world, not creating more."

"That was about cleaning up after stinky, hopeless men you could never change. Having a baby is about making new hope."

Jeff found these conversations deeply disturbing. They had

disagreed about things before, but only to the point where the person with the ambivalent feelings decided that the person with the stronger feelings was right. In five years, they had never actually had a fight—no raised voices, no slamming doors—and they considered that to be evidence of the flaw-lessness of their match.

But as this discussion about babies went around and around, night after night, Jeff began to see that there was no mutually satisfactory conclusion. Arguing with Angie about this was like telling a tidal wave bearing down on you to change direction. His cool logic was puny before the task. Yet his objections were not actually logical. Logically, he could see that plenty of people had babies and derived happiness from them. But, as deeply and as irrationally as Angie seemed to feel that a baby was going to be It, the key to her ultimate fulfillment, Jeff sensed that having a baby would destroy his life.

No ultimatum had been given, but he could see it as con-cretely in his hands as if it had been delivered Federal Express: If he didn't give her the baby she wanted, she would find a man who would. And then his life would be destroyed any-way. And it really wasn't fair, because they had agreed on it up front: no kids.

So that is why Jeff believed that it was Angie who first be-trayed the pact. And that it was he who was going to be re-quired to pay the price, whether he went along with her or not. What he told himself at the time was that maybe she was right. Maybe their family would turn out to be as differ-ent from a traditional family as their marriage had been from a traditional marriage. That is what he hoped, anyway, when he finally decided to be the one who gave in.

Quilt square: Lover—The first time didn't count. The first
pregnancy, anyway, not the first intercourse, because she
wasn't sure whether it actually *was* the first intercourse, because there was that ambiguous episode with Rafe. The thing
with Charlie wasn't even one of her great passions, he was just
a nice guy from college who came from her home neighborhood, whom she went out with when she was home the summer after her freshman year. They drove east to Westerville
and sneaked onto the beach after dark. You had to be careful,
because the cops patrolled and kicked people off, so they
found a tiny cove behind boulders where they could not be
seen from the main beach. It was a gorgeous night, with a big,
bright moon, and the surf was pounding on the beach, the
waves crashing and spraying and then sucking themselves
back out into the blackness of the lake. The sound was
lulling, mesmerizing. They drank a bottle of red wine, and
soon they were kissing. That old warm, dreamy feeling enveloped Angie. Charlie's good, strong hands under her sweatshirt melted her flesh. She unzipped his jeans.

He pulled a little foil packet out of one of his pockets.

"Uhn-uhn," said Angie, pushing it away.

"We gotta use something," he said.

"No," Angie murmured. "I wanna feel you come." She
could imagine what it would feel like, how he would moan
and grip her hard, and the warm, dreamy feeling would shoot
right up inside her body and obliterate everything. She
grabbed the little foil package out of his hand and threw it
over his shoulder, into the rocks.

A week before she was due back at college, she awoke from
the dream. Her period hadn't come. Her breasts were tender.
She was crying constantly for no apparent reason. She didn't
bother doing a test. She just knew.

Suddenly, her life came into sharp focus. If her parents
found out, she would be screwed for the rest of her life. They

would try to make her have the baby, either with Charlie, or in some place where they would take the baby away from her and put it up for adoption. Either way, she would never get over it. Her parents always found out everything about her, eventually; her only hope was to work fast.

So no one but Charlie could know about it until it was over. She made Charlie meet her on a baseball field at night, miles from home. She didn't ask him what he thought. She just told him to get her half the money and arrange to borrow somebody's car.

As soon as she got back to school, she made the appointment. It was hard to make the call; she had trouble, when the voice on the other end said, "Hello," forcing any words out, especially that awful, choking word: *abortion*.

She couldn't talk to Charlie, either. He came over one night but she wouldn't let him into her room. He stood in the hall outside, pounding on the door, yelling, "Get out here, Angie. Goddammit, get out here!" over and over. Later, his roommate told her, he punched a hole in the wall of his house. But she just couldn't talk to anyone until this thing was over.

The place was clean and bright. They gave her a tranquilizer. A really nice lady took care of her, holding her hand, rubbing it, murmuring, "This is going to hurt a little bit," while they dilated her. It was all women. They vacuumed her out. In the recovery room they gave her a 7UP and a Mystic Mint cookie, and it tasted better than any meal she had ever eaten. She felt deeply happy in the recovery room, and she stayed there a long time, until finally the nice lady came over and said, "You probably ought to be going home now."

Charlie drove her back, stopping once so she could throw up the 7UP and the cookie. He was surprisingly nice about it, considering how mean she had been to him. Probably, he was relieved, too. "I'm sure it's normal, Angie," he said. "You've been holding a lot of tension inside." When they got back to campus, she rolled like a child all the way down a steep hill and lay at the bottom, looking happily up at the sky and trees. She was proud of the way she had pulled herself together and saved her own life; maybe now she would be able to escape the awful force of her parents' power.

Except that what happened was her parents found out, and never forgave her, and she fell into a deep depression, and it was several years—until she met Jeff—before she could let a man touch her bare skin again.

◆

Angie could see that Jeff wasn't totally on board this time. But there had been other times when he'd jumped on a little late, like the time she got him to quit BDCC, and everything had worked out for the best. They watched the little test stick turn blue together, and she tried not to worry that his "Hey, great!" sounded noticeably wimpy. He brought home a holistic pregnancy guide one of the first nights, and showed none of his typical frugality when she asked him for money to buy some funky maternity clothes.

But his heart wasn't in it. Some guys might think it cute that their wives started having pregnancy cravings, just like in the sitcoms. Angie would be sitting in the hot, hot apartment, staving off nausea with slices of bread, and suddenly she would realize: If she could just go to an air-conditioned coffee shop and have a bowl of soup, she would feel great. But when she mentioned it, Jeff would just look at her with disgust in his eyes. Like it was okay to go out when they wanted to have fun, but he couldn't stand to look at her naked need.

They didn't do any of the stuff you're supposed to do as a couple. They didn't debate names, because Jeff wasn't very interested. They didn't shop for baby furniture, because Jeff thought that was a waste of good money; they found a beat-up dresser in a dumpster, and they didn't need a crib because Angie had read in *Mothering* about "family beds" and thought having the baby sleep with them would make it feel warm and welcome and safe. And they didn't bother with Lamaze, which Jeff said was just a bunch of scared people sitting around telling one another that it doesn't hurt.

In fact, at exactly the time when they might have been expected to start nesting, Jeff developed a wild enthusiasm for the idea of communal living. They had talked about it before, and agreed that it made a lot of sense, but somehow the opportunity had not actually presented itself until this pregnancy. Linda and Monique, who were part of their circle of friends from the neighborhood, were interested in finding an apartment with them, but then Linda decided she couldn't afford it and dropped out, so they ended up in a two-bedroom with Monique.

Angie was not entirely comfortable with this situation. She knew Jeff was fascinated with Monique. She was French, and Jeff thought anything European was automatically more interesting than anything American. He was also personally attracted to Monique, Angie could see that clearly. Not that this was a threat, because Jeff was far too upright to ever act on it, and besides, Monique actually seemed more interested in Angie than she did in him. Still, the hormones of pregnancy make you oversensitive to things like that.

Monique was always trying to get Angie to talk about relationships and really personal stuff. She would brew her unbelievably strong French coffee and curl her small catlike body into the rocking chair and fix her sharp, intense brown eyes on Angie and begin: "So, tell me how things go with you." And Angie, who normally liked this kind of conversation, felt herself battening down the hatches, doing anything she could think of to deflect Monique from direct inquisition. In the process, she learned quite a bit about Monique, such as the affair she'd had with a Chinese Ph.D. candidate whose wife and kids had gone back to China to spend some months with the wife's dying mother. But Monique had continued to hang around even after the family returned to Westerville, trying to befriend the wife, until finally she had been kicked out.

Honestly, Angie would have preferred not to share their space at this exact time. But she saw how badly Jeff wanted to, and it seemed to her that this was what people meant when they said marriage could be hard work. He had gone along with her pregnancy even though he hadn't wanted to, so now the least she could do was go along with the shared apartment.

And actually, she told herself, it was awfully progressive, the kind of thing she could see herself writing up for *Mothering* someday: "Parenting Among Friends: Life in a Communal Space." She could picture the three of them taking turns picking up the baby, just as they took turns getting the coffee. It was another sign of how they would refuse to allow parenthood to interfere with their commitment to alternative values.

Quilt square: Student—After the abortion, she just couldn't focus on anything, and she pretty much stopped going to classes. Except the women's studies class. And that was a departure for her, because in the late seventies the idea of women's studies was still pretty new and radical, certainly the kind of thing her parents would have disapproved of because what kind of a job was it going to get you after graduation?

But here was the amazing fact about women's studies: It was the only class Angie had encountered in college that had

anything to do with Real Life. What life was supposed to be
about, and why. Philosophy was supposed to teach you that,
but philosophy was actually about a bunch of guys sitting
around in a room trying to decide if the table they had their
feet up on really existed or not. But women's studies explained
so much: why you felt so angry and ashamed when guys whis-
tled at you on the street, why TV and advertising were so sat-
urated with images of half-naked women that also made you
feel angry and ashamed, why having an abortion was a decision you had a perfect moral and legal right to make for yourself. In Betty Friedan's *The Feminine Mystique*, with its
descriptions of desperate suburban housewives, Angie
thought she recognized her mother, and for the first time got
some inkling of why her mother kept getting sucked into that
big emotional black hole. Her mother's life seemed to be
mostly about trying to stay out of the hole, but there must be
some idea more positive than that to base a life on.

The class met in the evening, which made it seem more relaxed and intimate than the classes squeezed into the whorl of
daytime activity. And the people looked completely unlike
most of the people you saw on campus, budding jocks and
Farrah Fawcett–wannabes. They were what Angie would
come to think of as Alternative People, boys and girls (or, as
they were encouraged to call themselves, men and women)
dressed alike in jeans and tee shirts, with long straight hair,
the girls with no makeup and, Angie thought, very little pre-
tension. She was particularly fascinated by a woman who rode
a Harley-Davidson to class and said men were always offering
to pick the bike up for her, but she made a big deal about always picking it up herself. She thought she would have several
marriages, she said, or several serious relationships with men,
because she thought that, while she was a certain kind of person at this age, she would gradually change and grow and re-

quire a different kind of mate. They were encouraged to talk about things like that, personal things, in addition to reading about woman suffrage and the history of birth control.

The morning of the final exam, Angie's friend Pam was in really bad shape over some guy she'd broken up with. Angie thought she might even be suicidal. So Angie talked her down, and she was late for the exam and didn't have time to finish it. She knew it looked bad, coming in late like that, like she had no respect for the class, which definitely wasn't true. She wanted to write a note at the bottom of the exam to say that, and to say how important the course had been in getting her through her own bad time, because she knew she hadn't said much in class and it probably hadn't come across. But she didn't want to look like she was brownnosing, so she didn't do it. And in the end, she only got a C in women's studies.

The birth was horrible. Forty hours of painful, frightening labor, culminating in a cesarean. They cut her open and pulled the baby out and it felt like *bluh, bluh, bluh,* like pulling something out of Jell-O. She had a creepy sense of having felt this before, and suddenly remembered: the abortion.

But this time she had Jeff with her, and he really came through. The most romantic moment was when the midwife sent him out to eat some lunch, and he came back reeking of greasy hamburger, and there was no way on earth he would normally have chosen to eat a big hunk of red meat like that. He must have been beside himself, anxious to be back by her side. He breathed with her, pushed with her, soothed her; and when he came to find her in the recovery room afterward, he was holding a bunch of flowers.

A week later, they held hands as the midwife gave them a little going-home-from-the-hospital speech:

"You see, you have a little dollhouse that you live in, and when a baby's born, it's like some very big person comes along and picks up the dollhouse and shakes it, and all the furniture and the little people get knocked over, and the bed is in the kitchen and the bathtub is in the living room, and everything's just all mixed up, and it's your job to figure out where everything goes again."

They smiled at each other and thanked her. They knew they were going to be all right now, because they had faced something devastating and come out profoundly united; not since college had they been so much as one.

But from the word go, Angie had trouble implementing the *Mothering* philosophy. She was nursing, naturally, and she had read enough to know that the cardinal rule was, No relief bottles for four to six weeks, or the baby might learn to prefer the lazy ease of the plastic nipple to the relatively hard work of the real one.

So the first night in the hospital, when her roommate announced that she was going to let the nurses give her baby a bottle at night in the nursery so she could get some rest, Angie was torn. After almost two solid days and nights of labor, sleep sounded very tempting. On the other hand, that's why the *Mothering* people were so down on hospitals: You didn't want the baby picking up bad habits you wouldn't be able to break at home.

So the first night Angie asked the nurses to bring him in for demand feeding, and, sure enough, just as she was finally falling asleep for the first time, in he came, looking wide awake and ready for action. The next day, she had a long talk with Jeff, who told her, "You need some sleep. A couple of nights with a bottle isn't going to kill him." So the next night, she told the nurses to keep him in the nursery. "You deserve this," she reminded herself, but inside, a nagging little voice told her she had already begun to fail.

Also, the "family bed" was a disaster. They lay there, rigid and frozen, terrified they might roll over and crush Gabriel by mistake. Eventually, they would fall asleep, and then Gabriel would wake up to nurse, so they would both wake up, and Angie would take the baby into the living room for the feeding so Jeff wouldn't be kept up, but then sometimes Gabriel wouldn't go back to sleep and he'd cry and she'd be afraid to keep him in the living room where Monique might hear them and wake up, so she'd take him back in bed, and Jeff would wake up, and it could go on like that for hours.

One night, Jeff finally said, his voice tight with frustration, "Angie, I've *got* to get some sleep. I'm just going to go out and sleep on the living room sofa."

"Oh, come on, Jeff," Angie whispered urgently. "What about Monique? If she sees you sleeping out there, like you got kicked out of bed, she's gonna hand me a cup of coffee tomorrow and start in with, 'So, everysing iss well wiss you and Jeff?'"

"I'll handle it," Jeff said, heading for the door with his pillow. "I'll be back in here before she wakes up, or I'll just tell her what happened."

Then Angie lay awake, even after Gabriel fell asleep, worrying about whether Monique would see, what Jeff would say, what Angie would have to say, anyway, because Jeff couldn't really deal with personal conversations and would be bound to leave the wrong impression. Why did they need this, on top of the stress of just getting up with the baby?

In the morning, she had a long talk with her mom on the phone. Before the birth, she had pictured how her mom would drive out to Westerville a couple of times a week and help Angie out, and how this now-shared experience of motherhood would be a source of comfort and closeness for them. But her mother wouldn't come. She said the apartment, which was what Westerville realtors referred to as "vintage," was dirty and old and made her feel uncomfortable. Since Gabriel was born, she'd only come to visit once, and that was the *last* time Angie had called her in tears, because none of her prepregnancy clothes fit and she couldn't stand her maternity clothes and looking at her chubby body in the mirror made her so depressed she couldn't stand it. So her mother had run right over with a bag of her own clothes, jeans and polyester shirts like you would buy in Sears or Penney's if you were a middle-aged lady. Angie had put on one outfit and looked in the mirror. Presto: Instant Middle-Aged Lady. Instant "You Have Turned Into Your Mother." And then she had burst into tears all over again.

But this time her mom really came through. There was an old crib in the basement they could have. "And it's no wonder you're depressed, living in that dirty old apartment, with no privacy," she said. "There are new places out in the western suburbs that are twice as big and half as expensive. And you get nice new carpeting and a washer and dryer, too."

"But what about our lease?" said Jeff. "What about Monique?"

"I'll take care of subletting the apartment," Angie said. "That way she doesn't get stuck with the rent or new roommates, she just has to find somewhere else she wants to live."

"But how's she going to feel? It's like we're rejecting her friendship."

"I'll take care of it, Jeff. Look, this is a sucky way to raise a family. I mean, how about how *we* feel? This is *our* life."

"Okay, okay," said Jeff, thinking: "You mean, this is *your* life."

◆

Quilt square: Earth Mother—The best part was when you
were expecting. Angie had had a hot little body, but she didn't
at all mind watching it swell as the baby grew. It was like
watching yourself fill up with hope and power, knowing you
were everything to this little human being, that you were the
source of life itself, and you gave it all wordlessly, without
needing to be asked. This really *was* It—The Answer—the
ultimate unity with another, the ultimate sense of spiritual
and physical fulfillment. There was only one unfortunate as-
pect: It did not last forever. Sooner or later, you actually
birthed the baby, and the baby started wanting things you
might or might not want to give, and there you were, back in
the same old tug-of-war.

◈

Watching her belly expand, witnessing her preoccupation
with her own bodily functions, Jeff experienced, although he
was never consciously aware of it, the same dismay that Angie
felt as she watched him get carried away by BDCC. An exclusive romance, the province of only one partner, when both
partners have promised to share everything. But he recognized that this was not a fair or healthy response to the cre-
ation of one's own child, and so he tried to make himself
think positively of the thing to come: the sweet-faced, docile
infant who, as Angie insisted, would intuitively understand
how earnest and loving they were, how determined to be unlike their own parents, and would therefore coo and burble
cooperatively.

However, Gabriel arrived home wailing. Day or night, he
didn't care, nor did he care that other adults, unrelated to him
by blood, might not appreciate having their peace and sleep
shattered at random but frequent intervals. Monique tried to

be nice about it, but in neighboring apartments people pounded on the floors and ceilings, yelling, "Shut that baby up!" Only one thing—two actually—would do the trick, and Angie carried those around affixed to her chest. When it was Jeff's turn to take him, he'd let Gabriel suck on the flesh of his arm until a little welt was raised there, both of them waiting with equal desperation for Angie to bring the Real Things back.

This, for Jeff, was exactly like discovering that the boys in the Catholic high school didn't want to rap with him. He could tell himself rationally that babies cry, but his response to the way Gabriel cried was totally irrational. It stabbed at something half dead and buried deep within him, something still painful and tender and unwilling to be touched. Perhaps it was the anger he felt toward Angie for dragging him through this, or it might have been layers of anger laid down years before that, in a long-forgotten dump, like Schliemann's Troy, where layers could no longer be dated with much certainty. All he knew was that his reaction was so physical that he couldn't stop or control it, and he felt he could not safely be left alone with Gabriel. His dead-end programming job, which had always been the thing he did to make money so he could come home and live his Real Life with Angie, became his sanctuary. He still left work promptly at five, but he began to find that he could not drive past the entrance ramp where 94 West hurtled off toward Wisconsin without fantasizing what it would be like to simply circle off to the right and follow it.

In the nice, new, two-bedroom apartment in the far-western suburb with the nice, new, neutral-colored carpeting, Jeff had a flash of insight. As a cynical adolescent, he had assumed people lived in the suburbs because they *liked* it, because of some defect or mutation of taste that made them find it satisfying. But now he could definitely see how, once you had the kid, it made sense to have all that space and privacy, so you wouldn't inflict your chaos on others. And you needed those big expensive appliances because laundering your poopy (was he really *using* that word?) cloth diapers in the shared basement machine was a huge hassle. And once you were in the suburbs you needed the car to get anywhere, and he could start to see, not far over the horizon, barbecues and the PTA and the Boy Scouts.

Once you accepted the child, everything else fell right into place. But he still felt pretty dazed about it, like a driver in shock staggering away from a car accident, wondering what to do next. And Angie was so busy being pissed at him because he wasn't "coparenting" like the guys in that magazine she always read, that she didn't even try to understand his feelings. He came home from his stupid job and she was unavailable to him and Gabriel was full of needs he couldn't fill. He wasn't getting anything out of work and he wasn't getting anything out of home. So, if they were going to live in the suburbs anyway, what was the point of keeping up some pretense of being spiritually superior? His old friends at BDCC kept telling him he'd be welcome back anytime—in fact, they'd be willing to give him the same level job he'd have there now if he'd never left.

Angie got really upset when he told her about it. "You'll have to work ridiculous hours," she said. "You'll never be here."

"I'll get up extra early," he promised. "You won't really miss me in the morning, and I'll still come home the same time. And if it turns out you can't handle it, I'll just quit."

What could she say? She had gotten the baby, so he had gotten the place with Monique, so she had gotten this place, so now it was his turn. She didn't quite understand how this thing had happened—how, by each getting the things they most wanted, they had both ended up in exactly the place they had resolved together never to go: the conventional American suburban marriage. It was like that thing the ancient Greeks used to say about how guys who try to run away from their fate end up running right smack into it. Beneath Jeff's offer to accommodate her, Angie distantly sensed what he had sensed about her desire to get pregnant: that it was nonnegotiable. There are so many ways people can live together in holy matrimony and be unfaithful and say they aren't, or think they aren't, or think that because the other person already has been, that further infidelity is therefore justified. She didn't articulate it in her mind, but in her heart she saw what he had understood a year ago about her: that some big part of him had already left.

Quilt square: Daughter—Her mother always told the kids that honesty was the best policy (even though they almost always ended up in trouble when they told *her* the truth about anything). And her mom was always incredibly honest about her own feelings. Angie was her particular confidante, the one she told about all the suicide attempts: the time she had once contemplated jumping off a highway overpass, but decided against it, because it might cause an accident and someone could get hurt; the many long nights she had lain awake in bed hearing voices that told her to slash her wrists, and how sometimes Angie's dad had to hold her down for hours. And she talked about how many pills she could swallow at one time, in a weird way that sounded almost like bragging. She chattered about these things, and Angie guessed that she maintained a casual tone in order not to overburden Angie, to reassure her that even though it sounded so bad, it was still really okay, within the realm of Normal.

So Angie did not panic the first few times she felt the strange tingling in her own wrists as she lay in the dark next to her sleeping husband. Wasn't it odd, the way she heard those voices telling her, "Cut them"? Where was it coming from? It made no sense. It was the kind of thing that would happen to you if you were depressed, but Angie wasn't depressed. She wasn't sad. She could still remember the sight of her mother sliding down that wall, sobbing, into the very heart of sadness, into the big black hole. And surely those were the kinds of feelings that would make someone want to die. But Angie didn't feel anything like that. She didn't feel anything at all. She had a baby, she took care of it, she was coping just fine.

So she entertained the voices in her head, like uninvited but insistent guests, but she tried not to take them very seriously, and, for a long time, she didn't tell anyone else that they were there.

"The thing about having a baby is, you can never go backwards again," Angie said, handing me a mug of apple-cinnamon spice tea. "If we were going to give away everything we owned to try to start over again now, in addition to the trunk and the sewing machine and the backpack, we'd still end up with a crib, a trunkful of Gabriel's clothes, a trunkful of cloth diapers, a trunk full of Fisher-Price toys, a suitcase full of Tupperware snack containers and juice cups with sipper tops—you know what I'm saying? It just weighs you down."

Outside, flakes of snow sifted down from the gray afternoon sky, but inside it was warm and the tea was rich and fragrant, and I was basking in the luxury of this intimacy, because I knew exactly how long and lonely my winter would have been without it.

"Angie, you're more stripped down now than you've ever been in your entire life," I said.

"How can you say that? All I do all day is pick up the Duplos and put them in the Duplo box, and pick up the Waffle Blocks and put them in the Waffle Blocks box." Saying it, her eyes lit on the Duplos the kids had dumped out on the living room rug before running into Gabriel's room, and she squatted down to shovel them into a container with her hands.

"I'm not talking about material things. People divest themselves of material baggage as a sort of metaphor for divesting themselves of spiritual baggage, but having a baby does the same thing faster and much more efficiently." I thought for a moment about my own situation, and added, "Or maybe it doesn't get rid of the baggage, but it sure lays it out right in the open where you can't pretend anymore that you don't see it. Don't you think? I feel like I give every scrap of energy and consciousness I have to Sam, and all that's left over is exactly who I am, without any of my aspirations or intentions to pretty it up. And I'm sure when Ellis looks at me naked like that, he doesn't always like what he sees, and I know when I look at him naked like that, I don't always like what I see, either."

"Yeah," said Angie. "I know what you're saying. But I still don't see why it has to be like that. Look at Grace and Michael. I mean, it seems like if the man would really *help* the woman instead of running away, you wouldn't have this big drain of energy and everyone would be happier."

It was not an official playgroup day. Angie had been offering for weeks to cut Sam's hair, and I had finally decided to take her up on it. But as long as the kids were willing to play together in Gabriel's room and leave us to talk, we would seize the opportunity. Angie especially, I thought, seemed to need to talk. From the moment I walked in she struck me as unusually agitated, jumpy. I got the feeling there was something particular on her mind, and when Angie got like that she usually had to talk herself around in narrowing concentric circles before she could come to the point.

I was also procrastinating about the actual haircut. It was one of those irrational things that wouldn't make any sense to a person without a child, or a person with her second child, but somehow this first cutting of my first child's wispy auburn baby curls seemed momentous to me, a loss of innocence—as every small loss of innocence, from the first solid food to the first tooth to the first step, seems disproportionately momentous with the first child. I was afraid to cut it myself, having been raised in the kind of family that regarded skills of the hands—such as haircutting, sewing, and home repair—as impenetrable mysteries best left to those (in the lower classes) who have been trained to deal with them. However, I also couldn't bring myself to pay eight dollars for a professional cut, since despite my aristocratic values I had only a lower-middle-class bank account. It wasn't that Angie knew anything in particular about haircutting, just that she was braver and more casual about it than I was, and had been practicing on Jeff for many years. So it was a giant leap of faith for me to agree to let her do it; I cared deeply enough about having it done right that eventually I would have coughed up the eight dollars whether we could afford it or not, and to agree to Angie's offer was a conscious decision on my part to value her friendship above my snobbery.

"You want some more tea?" Angie asked, jumping up and going halfway to the kitchen before I could respond.

"It's okay, Angie. This is still almost too hot to drink."

"Well, I'll just heat up the water so it'll be ready when you want some more," she called from the other room. She came back a minute later, sat down next to me on the couch, got up again, and resettled herself across from me in a chair. Then she took a deep breath and said, "So."

"So," I repeated, smiling, to encourage her.

"So I've been thinking about what you said the other day at Café Espresso, about your fantasy of what you'd be doing if you'd never had a kid. And it made me think about what I'd be doing."

"And what would you be doing?"

"Well, what I decided was, that I'd be having a lot more sex."

"Wouldn't we all," I said, with a little snort. "But you know, I bet this is just a temporary thing. Once the kids get older, I'm sure we'll all get back to normal."

"Well, normal for us was never really that great."

"Really?" I said, Geraldo-like, unable to stop myself.

"Well, it was much better with Jeff than with anyone else

before him. I've got all that Catholic guilt stuff laid on really thick, you know? Like, the moment it starts feeling the teeniest bit good you get so terrified that you practically just pass out."

I laughed.

"No, I *mean* it. Sometimes I really feel right in the middle of it like I'm about to faint. And Jeff was the first guy who ever made me feel safe enough to just relax a little. But even then, I was always thinking about the abortion I had, and whether I might get pregnant again, so mostly we tried to do stuff other than intercourse."

Like what? I wondered.

"But now I feel like I wish I'd fooled around more before I married him. And even since we got married, I keep getting attracted to all these other men."

A little red flag went up in my mind. Suddenly I recognized her restlessness as the keyed-up state of a high school girl with a crush on someone, and I knew that was what she wanted to tell me about, and I knew that I didn't want to hear it. I liked Jeff a lot. Ellis and I had an ongoing problem, in our friendships with other couples, of our always liking only the husband or only the wife, and eventually we kept having to give those relationships up because the person who always got stuck with the bum spouse would start getting very irritated. But in this case, both of us liked both of them, and I didn't want to be a party to any confidences that were going to put me in the uncomfortable position of feeling I was an accessory to the betrayal of Jeff.

"Really," I said as coolly as I could. "If I were attracted to a man other than Ellis, I would just try to ignore it. There isn't any point in indulging that kind of thing, even in your own mind."

"Yeah," she sighed, "but it's not like something I can control. I just get totally carried away by it. You know, I've come real close once or twice to doing something about it, but then it would turn out the guy was afraid it would mess up my relationship with Jeff."

"Well, wouldn't it?" I had stopped drinking my tea, which was cold, and I could hear my voice growing colder as well.

"Oh, no. I always tell Jeff about it when I have a crush on someone, and he doesn't mind at all."

"And you believe that?"

"Yeah. He just jokes about it." Angie seemed oblivious to my discomfort. On the contrary, she was clearly warming to the subject and the great relief of confession. "We were just talking about it the other night, in fact, because it hasn't happened in such a long time, not since I got pregnant with Gabriel, but Jeff was saying, 'Yeah, I already guessed. I can always tell with you, and I know your type.'"

Suddenly, another, larger red flag went up in my mind. I heard an echo of Angie asking me about the kind of movies Ellis liked, and how he dressed for work, and why he'd gotten his ear pierced for his thirtieth birthday, and of the time she confided that sometimes she said his name over and over to herself, because just the sound of it was somehow so cool. So of course I had known for a long time now that the man Angie had a crush on was Ellis, and had tolerated it as long as it remained unspoken, because that is the kind of thing that sometimes happens among friends, and the kind of thing friends try to overlook so that the friendship can go on.

But for some reason, she didn't *want* me to overlook it. For some reason, I could tell she was about to describe her feelings to me in loving detail. She was still talking, telling me how many previous crushes there had been, naming the men so she could count them on her fingers, she thought there were four—wait—five, counting the newest one. "Oh God," I thought, "just please stop before you actually come out and say his name and maybe we can somehow come out of this with our friendship intact."

"I think we should check on what the kids are up to," I said, jumping up and lurching toward the hallway.

Angie followed me. "Oh," she said. "I almost forgot about cutting Sam's hair."

I didn't want her to touch his hair. But my mind had gone completely blank. If I just bolted, I'd have to say why, and then there would have to be a confrontation, and I wanted to avoid a confrontation at all costs. So I watched Angie sit Sam down on the closed toilet seat and wrap a towel around his neck, while I stood by, fidgeting with a comb. She wetted down his hair with a spray bottle, then brought out a pair of short, sharp shears. She kept trying to get him to hold his head still, while Gabriel danced around them, giggling and trying to distract Sam. I watched her hands going snip, snip, snip, and his soft, copper-colored curls dropping to the tiled floor, and the small loss of innocence seemed magnified and newly sinister. My idea of intimacy was drinking herbal tea together and letting her touch my child's hair. Her idea of intimacy was sharing her erotic feelings for my husband.

She turned to me and began again. "So Jeff thought it was really funny that he already guessed who it was."

She was desperate for me to ask. And I was equally desperate not to hear. I thought that as long as I could cling to the idea that I might have misunderstood her, it would be possible not to destroy our relationship, and with it the playgroup.

"We have to go," I said, finally.

"But I don't think it's really straight around the bottom."

"It looks fine." I pulled the towel off and took Sam into my arms.

"You seem kind of quiet today," Angie said as I tugged on Sam's jacket and then my own. "Is everything okay?"

"Fine," I said, dragging Sam out into the hallway. "I'll give you a call."

In the vestibule, I dropped Sam into the stroller. Then I ran the whole two blocks home. I felt that I had just smacked my head hard against the rock bottom of this friendship that was only two months old; whereas in a solid friendship, it might take years to find the bottom. I would no longer trust Angie as the disinterested consultant to my most personal problems. And didn't that make our friendship, and the play-group, worthless? But I couldn't imagine going back to my former isolation. This was who I was now, on the days when I was not a Writer: I was a lonely Mother, who could not bear excommunication from my community.

Nevertheless, I was relieved when Sam came down with strep, followed by the flu, and we had an excuse not to play with anyone for a few weeks, until we went east for the holidays. So I didn't see Angie again until January, and by then I had cooled off somewhat, and found I could manage a forced cordiality. I was careful for several more months not to be left alone in a room with her, and I think by then she was too preoccupied with other concerns really to notice.

CHAPTER 4

PARENTING STORY

GRACE

[Middle-class mothers] have made "love" of supreme importance in their relation to the child, theirs for him and his for them, partly because of the love complex of our time. . . . The child's need for love is experienced precisely because he has been conditioned to need it . . . conditioned to a slavish emotional dependence. . . . Not the need for parental love, but the constant threat of its withdrawal after the child has been conditioned to the need, lies at the root of the most characteristic modern neuroses.

Sociologist Arnold Green, quoted by Betty Friedan in The Feminine Mystique, *as evidence that full-time mothering can be harmful to children as well as to their mothers*

[W]hen a child's development is arrested, when feelings are repressed, especially the feelings of anger and hurt, a person grows up to be an adult with an angry, hurt child inside of him. This child will spontaneously contaminate the person's adult behavior. . . . I believe that this neglected, wounded inner child of the past is the major source of human misery.

John Bradshaw, from Homecoming: Reclaiming and Championing Your Inner Child

The Pygmies are the living evidence of our innate goodness. In a world threatened by oppression, conflict, and violence, these forest people demonstrate that when we gently birth, nurture, and guide our children without repressive controls, human beings can live together in freedom and harmony.

Ushanda io Elima in "Life with the Pygmies," in Mothering *magazine, Summer 1988*

■ ■ ■

It was their perception from the beginning that baby Phoebe was an exceptionally challenging infant. This perception was reinforced by the comment of the nurse who brought her back to Grace's bedside after the night that first week in the hospital when Grace had finally, exhausted and torn by guilt, sent her to the nursery. "Lemme tell you," the nurse said, handing the red-faced, wailing Phoebe over to Grace for breast-feeding, "this kid *never* sleeps."

Grace spent a lot of time in the first three months trying to match Phoebe to the descriptions of normal infant behavior in a range of child-care books. Newborns were said to need at least eighteen hours of sleep in any twenty-four-hour period, but no matter how many times Grace added it up, Phoebe's never came out to more than twelve. She wondered if Phoebe had colic, which the books defined as crying for three hours inconsolably, but Phoebe would never cry for three hours inconsolably, because every hour and a half, Grace would offer her nipple and the little mouth would immediately latch on and quiet down. (The books said she was only supposed to be nursing at three- to four-hour intervals.) It was probable, Grace concluded, that Phoebe was what the older, insensitive books called a "fussy" or "demanding" baby, which the newer, more sensitive books had corrected to "High Need."

During [the first] year, the baby is never separated from the mother. This constant contact is . . . one reason why Pygmy infants rarely cry. Pygmy babies appear to feel good. They are satisfied in all of their requirements. On the rare occasions when a baby does cry, it is only for a moment, because immediately the child is given the breast.

After a nursing, there might be fifteen or twenty minutes of calm in which she could put Phoebe down, and quickly take a shower or eat lunch or return a phone call or open the mail. But then the wailing would begin again, and Grace would pick Phoebe up and try to distract her with a little tour around the apartment, letting her touch the radiator grate and feel its texture, stopping at the window to watch a curtain flutter in the breeze, whatever would make Phoebe focus her huge blue eyes with intense concentration for a few minutes, before she began to disintegrate into the wailing state. And then there would still be an entire hour left to be gotten through, the absolute minimal interval Grace felt she must maintain between feedings. (It was Phoebe's body, not the books, that Grace took as her cue on this subject. Phoebe clearly would have been happy to chomp away at a nipple every moment of the day, but letting her do it entirely on demand always resulted in copious amounts of curdled, yellowish regurgitation.)

The books said babies could just be put down for a nap, but Phoebe, put down in her crib while awake, became frantic, furious, desolate. She could fall asleep only while nursing. But nursing did not guarantee that she *would* fall asleep. There were many, many days when the hours of wailing would rub Grace's nerve endings raw, when Grace herself would become frantic, furious, desolate, when she felt she would do absolutely *anything* if Phoebe would just sleep one solid hour and let her have some peaceful time to herself. At the eleven A.M. nursing, the chant would run through Grace's head: Go to sleep, go to sleep, go to sleep. Sometimes Phoebe would fall only half asleep, and Grace would think desperately, "Maybe there's still a chance." So she would lay Phoebe gently in the crib, kneel down next to her, and pat her gently on the back: pat, pat, pat, go to sleep, go to sleep, pat pat pat; and as soon as she saw Phoebe really drifting off, she would verrrrrry slooooowly craaaaawl toward the door on her hands and

knees, careful not to make a sound. And she might get all the
way to the threshold, almost home free, and then CREAK
would go the floorboard and UP would pop Phoebe's tiny little head and WHAAAAAA would come the cry of the
abandoned child.

So of course Grace would go back and pick her up. It was
very important that Phoebe be satisfied in all her requirements. Grace's requirements would just have to wait, because,
after all, she was the grown-up. And anyway, no matter how
hard she tried she could never quite get a fix on what her own
requirements were.

So many solitary hours passed to the accompaniment of that
angry wailing. No friendly grandmas dropped in to take over
for a few hours—Grace's mother had been dead for five years,
and Michael's was back in Minneapolis. No curious, gossiping
friends—Grace's Chicago pals from grad school were all now
absorbed into the irregular life of the theater, or scattered to
other Bohemian enclaves across the country. And Grace was
really not a joiner, no exercise classes or support groups for
her; all those disposable diapers and disposable bottles and
chemically concocted formulas and all that materialistic chatter didn't make her feel supported, only more alienated, mar-
ginalized, stridently Alternative.

Sometimes when she couldn't stand it anymore she would
call up Michael at school.

"How you doing?" he would start out, sounding genuinely
concerned.

"Oh, she just doesn't stop crying. I'm so discouraged."

"Do you need me to come home right now?" She could hear
his voice tighten almost imperceptibly.

"Well, no, it's not that bad, it's just . . ." Her reply would trail off. Of course she would like him to come home right now.

The [Pygmy] father takes great interest in his baby. He plays, holds, and hugs the child as much as the mother does. Love and care are equally manifested by men and women.

"Because I'll come if you need me. I mean, this isn't a really great time, I'm supposed to talk to my adviser at three, but if it's an emergency, I'll come."

Now she could hear his annoyance clearly. And it was really quite justified. He already did so much. He'd stayed home full-time for the whole first six weeks while she lay in bed recovering from the faulty epidural, and he stayed home every Tuesday morning while she went to talk to the Jungian therapist to try to let go of her negative energy about the cesarean. (Pygmies have very short, natural, easy labors, even despite the fact that they have proportionally the biggest babies in the world.) He came home pretty much every evening at five and usually cooked dinner, and when he took over with Phoebe he *really* took over, he wasn't one of those fathers who take the baby and hand it back screaming fifteen minutes later, saying, "I think she really wants *you*."

"It's okay," she would say, only it wasn't, it was even worse now, because now he was mad at her, and the whole reason she had called him up in the first place had been her vague unarticulated hope that he would say something praising and loving about what she was doing, something about the enormous value of her self-sacrifice, the importance of her being there so their child would know only breast milk, would have a parent's love on demand, would not experience the psychic devastation of frustrated needs, would never know the conscious or unconscious cruelty that a hired baby-sitter—not wired into Phoebe by Nature Herself—might inflict in a moment of insensitivity. Yes, Michael did work very hard at fathering, but he also had this ongoing role in the Outside World, where he talked with and joked with and was taken seriously by other adults and did work that was considered important to the sum total of human knowledge. And he was managing to do *both* these things, whereas she, despite all of her best planning and her education and all of their feminist intentions, had ended up doing only this. *Only* this.

◈

Before the birth, they had very clearly discussed sharing the parenting and the outside work fifty-fifty. That had been part of the point of their choosing careers with such flexible hours, in academia and the theater.

So when, three months after Phoebe was born, Grace got a call from a theater school buddy asking her to direct a twenty-minute one-act, it seemed like the ideal way to wade slowly back into her career. Rehearsals could be scheduled in the evenings when Michael was home, in two-and-a-half-hour blocks, which was just about how long they could stretch Phoebe between nursings. It wasn't *ideal*, because usually at the beginning and end of the rehearsals you needed to talk about the costuming and the sets and the scheduling and other details, and Grace couldn't really stick around for any of that, but the actors were all old school friends and she felt that they understood her predicament.

And then it seemed that everything was just falling into place when, about three months later, she got an invitation to assistant-direct a production of *The Cherry Orchard* for the director's Chekhov class. It was such a big class that the director had split it into two separate casts, and Grace was to direct the second one. On the one hand, it was a great oppor-

tunity for Grace to meet some actors, make some new contacts, get her name out and around; on the other hand, this
was a bunch of strangers who did not understand or necessarily sympathize with her personal circumstances. She definitely
got the impression that the director, a gay man, did not approve of the way that, after exactly two hours, Grace would
point to her watch, apologize profusely, and rush out the
door, her breasts heavy, tingling, beginning to leak into the
cotton nursing pads in her bra, overflowing into telltale dark
circles on the chest of her shirt. Some rehearsals she didn't
even make it to, because of conflicts with Michael's schedule
or because they overlapped with Phoebe's bedtime nursing,
and for that she felt constantly guilty and insecure, because
who ever heard of a director not being at every rehearsal?

The final dress rehearsal went until almost midnight, and
then Grace was invited to go out for a drink with the whole
cast. She agreed to go along, even though Phoebe was still
waking up twice a night to nurse, and the first time would be
in about two hours. But it would be worth it, Grace thought,
because somehow that had always been the thing she loved
best about theater work, she who was so shy and reluctant to
reveal herself to strangers: It was the intense emotional work
with a group of people, the trust and bonding that developed,
a feeling like family but safer and more respectful than any
real family ever felt, and the glorious sense of release you got
when you finally drank and partied and let it all loose at a
purely social level. (Actually, that was how Grace had originally met Michael, when they worked together on the high
school production of *A Midsummer Night's Dream* sophomore
year; at the cast party, they had all drunk exorbitant amounts
of beer and wound up rolling around the floor in a series of
drunken tickle fights.)

So she went along for the drink, but in the bar she kept
finding herself glancing at her watch, thinking: "Only one

more hour until she's up; and then she'll be awake again three hours later." She couldn't get her heart into any of the conversation, and halfway through her beer she suddenly developed a violent stomach cramp, and wasn't sure she would be able to get up and walk to the car.

Driving back up Sheridan Road toward home, hunched over the steering wheel in pain, she reflected that you couldn't ask for a clearer sign. If her first priority was to be fully available to meet Phoebe's needs, she couldn't put herself in any more situations that made her feel so exhausted, so guilty, so torn. Besides the fact that Michael at the moment was having to work pretty much full-time to get up to speed on his dissertation, there was the other inescapable fact (somehow so insignificant-seeming before the actual birth) that only Grace could breast-feed.

She supposed a project might fall into her lap that was absolutely irresistible, that would justify the huge physical and psychological jolt of separation directing would produce in her relationship with this extraordinarily High Need baby. And in that case, maybe they'd work something out.

But nothing like that did just happen to fall into her lap, and her days with Phoebe disappeared one after another into the unending struggle to provide enough comfort and stimulation to keep Phoebe from screaming, and the respite she snatched from Phoebe's short, unpredictable naps was never sufficient for her to really concentrate her energy on going after a theater job, which after all would pay little if anything and only result in more disruption to all their lives.

So that was how it happened, without her quite deciding it *should* happen, that Grace became simply a stay-at-home mom.

◈

What did the Pygmy mommies do all day? They gathered berries together or wood for the fire or participated in the hunt alongside the men, the article said. They shared the same work, the same values, the difficulties of Pygmy life. All the grown-ups hugged and touched all the children; they did not appear to need pamphlets, in Pygmy society, to distinguish Good Touch from Bad Touch. The children called *all* the grown-ups "father" and "mother"; they followed all the grown-ups around, imitating them and learning the business of being a Pygmy. The Pygmy mothers gossiped and flirted and continued on as sociable, productive members of adult society even after bearing children. Pygmy society didn't seem to have bizarre practices such as scattering childbearing women in isolated huts throughout the forest and expecting them to emerge five years later, mentally serene, with children who were perfectly socialized, and reading-ready.

◈

Phoebe's fine motor skills were remarkably advanced. Grace encouraged them, of course, providing natural wood blocks for her to stack and educational Ravensburger puzzles, which Phoebe could complete at an amazingly precocious age. Privately, Grace worried about her gross motor development, however. Phoebe looked big and sturdy, but she was uncoordinated and extremely cautious; even though it was clear at fourteen months that she could walk independently, she chose not to, clinging to one of her parents' hands every single walking moment until she was eighteen months old.

Grace tried to make every bit of her time with Phoebe quality time, but realistically, you couldn't go the ten straight hours, from the time Phoebe awoke until the time Michael came home from school, stacking blocks and finger painting, plus there was that unpredictable element of the nap that might or might not happen.

So Grace came to rely on an hour of *Sesame Street* every morning, even though she felt conflicted about how healthy it was. Because what did you really teach children by putting them in front of a TV set, except how to watch TV? And *Sesame Street*, for something that was supposed to be educational, was peculiarly self-referential, with practically all the skits based on dumb TV shows, so you wouldn't even get the joke unless you watched the dumb TV shows, too. And no one behind the scenes of this pointedly integrated program seemed to have noticed that practically every single interesting nonhuman character was male.

So no, it wasn't ideal, and it did make her feel somewhat irresponsible (at the same time, she was secretly proud of Phoebe's attention span, that she'd sit so quietly and really *concentrate* for that hour), but it couldn't be that ultimately destructive, could it? Because she'd watched things far worse than that in her own childhood, and it wasn't even as though her own mother had been standing by to lavish compensatory quality time on her afterward. Wasn't it funny, the way people drew this distinction between "working" mothers (assuming them to be absentees) and stay-at-home mothers (assuming them to be There for their children)? Whereas Grace could summon up quite vividly the pain of having a mother who stayed home for thirty-five years and was never There for her at all.

◆

Born in 1960, Grace was the last of her mother's six children, arriving fifteen years after the first. Mary had started her married life as a perfect post–World War II housewife, thriftily sewing her children's clothes, cooking elaborate casseroles straight out of the pages of women's magazines, and supporting her husband Peter's careers in law and local politics. There was a story about one of her pregnancies (but with so many, they'd lost track of specifically which one) where Mary had gone to the hospital to deliver the baby, bringing with her a tie she had hand sewn for Peter on which she had embroidered the words *IT'S A* so that she could instantly stitch in *BOY* or *GIRL* and Peter could put it on and get an adorable photo into the local paper for whatever political campaign he had been engaged in at the time.

But by the time Kate and then Grace finally came along, Mary had had it with the housewife routine. Dinner was a hunk of meat or fish you could plop in the oven and serve with frozen vegetables. The older kids helped set the table and wash the dishes, and a hired German woman came in several days a week to clean and cook. It was this German woman who gave them what mothering they got, who had the patience to bake bread and make doughnuts with them and really *play* with them. Mary didn't pay them much attention, except when they got underfoot and caught the brunt of her highly inflammable temper.

Mary didn't look like a respectable suburban matron by then, either. When Grace came home from school, she would be down in the basement in torn-up clothes, refinishing some piece of furniture she'd found for nothing in an antique store. The entire house (which Mary had designed; she had majored in architecture in college) was full of these finds. Sometimes Mary redecorated her friends' houses, and eventually, during the course of her years of haunting the antique shops, she picked up enough knowledge to begin researching a book on local silversmiths and jewelers. She spent hundreds of hours tracking down craftsmen's marks through old newspapers, re-creating them in sketches and photographing finished pieces.

When the book was published, it was dedicated to Grace and Kate, who were in grade school, and Grace always assumed that was because of the guilt Mary felt at having spent all that time on her own interests, at the expense of her maternal responsibilities toward her last two children.

◈

Phoebe, Grace had resolved, would never know the hard edge of a mother's unexplained and unsolicited anger. She could forgive her own mother, who had died of a brain tumor the summer Grace finished college, because Mary had lived before feminism, before Conscious Choice. Mary hadn't had a Career, she had had Projects; not a life of her own to which she was entitled, but a life she'd had to steal out from under her maternal responsibilities, and the price was this great guilt, which in turn spawned all that anger and resentment she ended up taking out on the children.

But things weren't like that anymore. We had lived through the birth control revolution, and read Alice Miller. We had the ability to choose or not to choose parenthood, to choose or not to choose careers, so we had no good reasons to feel angry and frustrated, especially given this acute consciousness of how much the parent's anger and frustration, whether expressed or repressed, could damage the psychological health of the child. Having chosen children consciously, we must parent them consciously. And we, who had such good, rational educations, had the full benefit of anthropology, sociology, psychology, Spock, and *Mothering* to help us know what to strive for.

[Pygmies] are not afraid. They are totally secure. They also have a high level of self-worth and self-respect. Most significantly, Efé Pygmies are free of hatred, greed, and competitive feelings.

But, oh, those Pygmy women. Life for them must be like one big cast party: lots of dancing and drumming, herbal intoxication; the glorious release of letting it all, letting IT ALL OUT. Those fortunate bare-breasted Pygmy women, they did not suffer this loneliness.

◈

After the spring thaw of the year Phoebe turned one, Grace began regularly taking her to the Tot Lot down the street. Phoebe literally clung to her every moment; still, being able to smile at other adult women while your child clung to you was measurably more morale-boosting than having your child cling to you in the isolation of your own home. You saw interesting-looking women in this part of Westerville, some of whom Grace privately targeted as future friends; but the conversations she actually had with those women were disappointingly brief and mundane.

Until Angie came along, and swept her off her feet. It was odd, but whenever she thought about it, that comparison to a dating relationship would pop into her mind, because the only times Grace had ever experienced the intensity of a relationship that built up so quickly and compellingly were in sexual situations with men.

It started out flirtatiously, when Grace arrived home one afternoon and discovered that the little yellow plastic bucket hanging off the stroller handle that looked exactly like Phoebe's bucket had a piece of adhesive tape on the bottom that said "GABRIEL" in big block letters. So the next time she ran into Angie in the Tot Lot, of course they had to make a date to exchange the buckets, and suddenly they were in the middle of one of those conversations of intense mutual recognition, where they both kept interrupting each other, amazed, to say "Me *too!*": Both of them had kept their own last names and used them as their children's middle names; and they both bought their children organic junk food, as opposed to Junky junk food; and they were both vegetarians; and then it came out that Angie had had a C-section, too, and had lots of the same feelings about her childbirth experience as Grace, who had been struggling with them alone.

What Angie kept asking her was "Why do you think that happened to you?" Her philosophy seemed to be that everything that happens is an opportunity for spiritual growth, so there must have been some way Grace had *needed* this birth experience in order to learn.

And that was a question Grace couldn't immediately answer, but it intrigued her, and she was intrigued by Angie for asking about it, so the more she thought about the question, the more she thought about the potential of this person who knew enough to frame the question. And suddenly she realized how hungry she was for a relationship like this, the way you would hunger for a man, because he made you suddenly feel noticed, when you had gone on for such a long time fully reconciled to being evermore merely part of the woodwork. Angie called her all the time, and sometimes just when she thought of calling Angie, but then decided, "No, it's too pushy, she wouldn't want to see me again already," Angie would call right then and propose another get-together. So very quickly they were seeing each other once a day, and then twice a day, meeting in the morning, going back to their respective apartments for two or three hours for lunch and nap time, and reuniting later at the beach or at the park.

For Grace, the really magical part was that finally she had found a way to spend time with Phoebe that was also time that she, Grace, got something valuable out of. Her needs and Phoebe's needs, for once in perfect harmony. She didn't have to worry that the intense conversations with Angie deprived Phoebe of attention, because Phoebe was getting the important socialization experience of being with Gabriel. Not that they always got along. Phoebe was definitely bigger and more aggressive than Gabriel, and Gabriel wasn't very good about standing up for himself. When Phoebe grabbed a toy away from him, he'd either grab it back and run away as fast as he could, or, more frequently, just stand there and start wailing, so an adult would have to intervene. And usually, Angie would just stand by and let Grace be the mediator, probably because she saw herself and Gabriel as the injured parties. That made Grace very self-conscious about how she handled things.

Hallet never saw a Pygmy adult hit or criticize a child. Nor do they tell their children how to act. When asked how they control their children, Hallet answered, "They don't. The children do not need to be controlled."

First, she would try to distract one or both of them by giving them a new toy, or proposing a new game. And if that didn't work, she would try out some compromise, like "You play with this for three minutes and you play with this, and then we'll trade." And if none of those things worked, then she might say, "Well, if we can't work out a compromise, then no one can play with it," and she'd take the toy away. What you wanted to steer clear of were words like *no* and *bad*—words that imposed frustration or negative labeling on the child. And you avoided anger, which would surround the whole issue with a negative emotional content, when, in fact, it was an opportunity to teach conflict-resolution skills. She looked constantly to Angie for feedback; she cared much

much more about what Angie felt in these situations than she did about Gabriel, and she could see that Angie usually looked miserable, but when she asked if there was some other way Angie thought they should handle things, she would only shrug.

Well, the children would outgrow these problems. Grace clung to a comment Angie had made after they had known each other only a few weeks. "I really see us as being old women together, sitting on the porch, rocking in our rocking chairs, while our grandchildren mess around in the organic vegetable garden." It was such a flattering, even *romantic* thing to say; their connection was intense, vital enough to outlast the inevitable facts of modern life, the transience, the corporate transfers, the way even your greatest friendships eventually dwindled into an annual exchange of Christmas cards.

It might, Grace suspected vaguely, be a friendship simply too good to be true. There were hints that Angie was a kind of Don Juan among women. One day at the beach, another kid started playing with Phoebe and Gabriel and their sand toys, and Angie got into a conversation with the kid's mother and discovered she was planning to send him to Waldorf School, and Angie seemed to find that deeply fascinating, and by the time the woman picked up her stuff and left, Angie had gotten her phone number and made a plan to come visit her house the next week.

Then she looked over at Grace, who had been quiet through this whole conversation, and whom Angie appeared to have temporarily forgotten. "Isn't that cool?" she said. "It should be really interesting to see what her house is like."

Grace, who hadn't really liked the woman, tried to remain open and neutral. "I'm just a little surprised that you jumped into that so quickly," she said.

"Well, it's so interesting when you meet a new person like

that, when you feel like you might really learn something from her. You don't want her to just get away and that's it."

"Well," said Grace, "I'm always a little afraid to make that initial involvement with people, because what if it turns out that you don't really like them, and you want to back out, but by then it's gotten awkward?"

"It doesn't have to be awkward," Angie said confidently. "I think if a relationship looks good, you just jump into it. Then, if you don't like it, you just jump out."

So that was there, in the back of Grace's mind, an annoying mosquito kind of thought that might bite or might eventually fly away. Grace heard it buzzing again when Angie went alone to that first playgroup meeting, and started to become fascinated with Nina, and all of a sudden started talking about how part-time work was The Answer and those *Mothering* people were fucked up to think that just by being there and controlling every second of your child's life you were going to avoid screwing up your kids just as badly as your own parents had screwed up with you.

But then there was that other thing in the back of her mind, the soothing image of the two weathered ladies rocking away old age in the kind of intimacy a man could never really share, and that was the image she tended to drift toward, because it got her through the long days on end when Michael was not around to help her carry a burden that she did not wholly enjoy carrying, did not always feel strong enough to carry by herself, but believed she could never, ever again lay down.

■ ■ ■

Grace was very worried about leaving Phoebe for two whole nights, but when she arrived to pick up Angie at her apartment Friday evening, Angie was all pumped up. She was dressed in funky, baggy pants and a shocking pink silk shirt, and she had on a pair of extra-long, dangly, silver-and-turquoise earrings.

"Want one?" she asked, when Grace admired them. She took out the left earring and handed it to Grace. "I got them to celebrate our Journey to Freedom."

Grace looped the earring into her right ear, and they stood arm in arm before the mirror, Grace so cool and light and muted, Angie dark and vibrant and intense.

"How come you never share your earrings with me?" Jeff said, coming to stand behind them.

"Get your ear pierced, like Ellis, and I will," Angie said. "How about it, Grace? It is too weird?"

It *was* weird, but in kind of a nice way, a very Angie way. But not, Grace decided, in a Grace way. "No thanks," she said, unhooking the earring. "It's kind of heavy. I'm not used to it, so it feels a little uncomfortable in my ear."

Angie shrugged, and went into the kitchen.

"Michael said to call if you get lonely for dinner tomorrow night," Grace told Jeff.

"Hey," said Jeff. "Don't worry about us. We're big, macho guys. We'll be fine."

Angie came back, carrying a stuffed paper grocery sack, which she thrust into Grace's arms.

"What's this?" asked Grace.

"Treats. For the Journey."

◆

Flying down Lake Shore Drive, past the jeweled Chicago sky-
line, Grace began to cat h some of Angie's exhilaration. It
was like being a teenager, finally released from the watchful
eyes of your parents.

"You know," Grace said, "in eighteen months, I haven't
spent one whole night away from Phoebe."

"It's too bad you couldn't do it some time with Michael,"
Angie said. "Maybe when Phoebe gets a little older, she could
stay with us and you guys could get away."

"That seems like such a fantasy."

"I know," said Angie. "You feel like, if you ever *did* get that
kind of privacy, you're not sure you'd remember what to do
with it anymore. You know how you could never buy into the
Catholic stuff, before you were married, where birth control
is: You just don't Do It? But that's definitely the system we've
used since we had Gabriel."

Grace laughed, but didn't match Angie's confidence. Instead, she said, "But you know, I don't think I could have done
this at all if Michael hadn't pushed me. I just feel so guilty
about leaving her."

"I wish Jeff would push me like that," Angie sighed. "I
could tell he didn't like this idea at all. He's just doing it because he makes all these business trips, and he feels like he
owes me. I feel guiltier about leaving him than I do about
leaving Gabriel."

So they launched quickly and happily into The Good Stuff,
as they circled down the Skyway, across northern Indiana,
and up the Michigan coast, toward the summer house on the
shore of the lake that had been in Grace's family for genera-
tions. Angie passed Grace hummus-filled whole wheat pita
pockets and then homemade zucchini bread from the Treat

bag, and they talked for the whole three hours. Wrapped in
the warmth of the little car, they both were drowsy by the
time they reached the house, huge and deserted in the November darkness.

The place was cold and unheated, and they decided to go
straight to bed. Grace led Angie up to the third-floor master
bedroom.

"This is the biggest bedroom, with the nicest view," she
said, "and this is where I usually like to sleep."

They looked for a moment at the double bed. Then Angie
said, "Well, it's big enough for two. Let's both sleep here."

So they both changed into their nightgowns, quickly, because it was so cold, and got into the double bed. Grace felt
an inexplicable sense of danger in the air. She lay in the darkness, not touching Angie but close enough to feel the warmth
of Angie's body, with the fleeting sense that something defin-
itive was about to happen. She didn't know whether she was
scared of it, or how she would react if it did happen. But then
she heard Angie's even breathing and realized she had gone to
sleep.

Eventually Grace began to drift off as well. She dreamed
that she and Angie were lying in the bed together, and that
Angie leaned over and kissed her.

In the morning, she told Angie about the dream, and
Angie laughed. So Grace laughed, too.

◈

That Saturday morning was cold and bright. Grace loaded up
her backpack with a jar of organic peanut butter, a hunk of
sharp white Cheddar cheese, a loaf of cracked wheat bread,
carrot sticks, and apples, and then she took Angie for a long
hike through the woods.

"This whole setup is so amazing," Angie kept saying. "The house, the woods, the privacy. I feel like, if this was in my family, I'd spend all the time here I could. I feel like I could really be creative here."

"Yes," said Grace, "but my brothers and sister use it, too, so we really have to take turns. And it's not real life here. If you lived here, you'd have to have a job, and all your real-life chores and complications, and then it would be just as stressful being here as being anyplace else."

They walked along for a while in silence. Grace felt a deep, soft happiness. Her guilt over Phoebe had faded, and she was able just to enjoy the half-forgotten peace of unbroken thought and conversation. And she was glad to be able to share this place with Angie.

She led them out of the woods, onto a desolate stretch of beach. The winter surf was pounding, and the day had grown slightly overcast, giving the beach a wild, lonely feel that Grace loved. She pointed to a big dune and said, "Let's have lunch up there."

"I'm kind of tired," Angie said. "Why don't we just stop here?"

"Because the view up there will be perfect," Grace said. "Come on, it's just a little farther."

Grace scrambled up quickly, and Angie struggled up behind her. At the top, she said, "Geez, Grace, all this exercise is making me kind of crabby."

Grace laughed, and told her about the time she and Michael had climbed up the mountain in Japan, when Grace was in the first trimester of pregnancy. It was August, and August in Japan was just as bad as August in Chicago, only the Japanese weren't into shorts and halter tops. You weren't supposed to go into the holy places unless you were pretty well covered up. Grace and Michael wanted to hike to the top of this holy mountain in Kyoto, and they anticipated it would take about an hour and a half, so they set out early with a small bottle of water, expecting to get all the way up before the sun came out full blast.

But they had underestimated. The temperature was well into the nineties by the time they were still only halfway up, and they had already drunk the water, and both their shirts were soaked with sweat.

They stopped and sat down for a moment, wondering if they should just turn around. But then the whole morning's effort would be wasted. "Just keep thinking about how good it will feel to be at the top," Michael said. And so, up they went, visualizing their arrival, staggering a little toward the end.

At the very top of the holy mountain, they found a soda machine, and a whole bunch of American tourists just getting off a trolley that had run up the other side of the mountain.

"Wow," said Angie. "I bet you were really pissed off. So did you take the trolley back down?"

"Oh, no," said Grace. "As soon as we had the sodas, we felt better, and we laughed about it, and we decided if we could get up, we could get down, because going down is always easier."

Angie regarded her for a moment with that frown of concentration she always made when some column in her mind wasn't tallying properly. "What makes you *be* like that?" she said. "Why do you want to push yourself so much?"

Grace thought about it for a moment. "I guess because it doesn't necessarily feel like pushing. It just feels like going somewhere."

"I feel like there's a piece I must be missing," Angie said. "Because to me it just feels like pain. When it starts hurting, I just want to stop doing it. In college I was pretty athletic, and Jeff always said I could be a really good runner if I was willing to train, but it's so much effort, why would I want to?"

She watched Grace spread out a blanket and begin to unpack the food, but she seemed to be listening to something going on very faintly within her own mind.

"It's kind of how I feel about this motherhood stuff," she continued. "Like, I thought it was going to be so easy and natural, and I was always going to know just what to do. But I feel like my instincts are always wrong."

"In what way?" asked Grace.

"Well, did I tell you that I talked to my brother and sister-in-law a couple days ago, and she was like, 'It's wrong for you to vaccinate Gabriel'?"

She waited for Grace to comment, but Grace merely listened, so she went on: "So what's wrong with it? I did a lot of research into it, and I decided it was better to go ahead and do it."

"Well," said Grace, "then you made the choice that was right for you."

"Well," said Angie pointedly, "then why don't you vaccinate Phoebe?"

"Because that's our choice. Because we've decided that there's a lot of risk involved, and the necessity for vaccination doesn't outweigh the risk."

"It *isn't* that dangerous," said Angie. "*Mothering* makes it sound like it is, but when you look at the statistics, it's only a teeny percentage of kids that have reactions."

"Yes, but what if it happens to be *your* kid? Anyway, just because we don't believe in it for us, doesn't mean you can't do it yourself. *They* may disapprove of you, but I honestly don't."

They ate for a while in silence. Then Angie said, "Does Phoebe ever do things that make you upset?"

"Oh, all the time," said Grace.

"No, I mean like, when she and Gabriel are together."

"Well, sometimes they don't get along that well," Grace conceded.

"Yeah, but don't you find that she can be sort of irritating? I don't really know how to explain it."

There was a pause, and Grace thought Angie was waiting for Grace to draw her out. But now suddenly Grace was feeling defensive, and she didn't think she really wanted to hear whatever it was that Angie was trying to express, so instead she began to wrap up the lunch leftovers.

"Let's start home," she said. "I'm cold."

◆

Grace felt better after the hike home, and they both took naps. Then Grace cooked spaghetti, and they made a fire and opened a bottle of wine and had a pleasant dinner, and she felt completely relaxed. She turned on some music and sat down on the couch, wondering if she could get Angie interested in a game of Scrabble.

But Angie sat down and began again, as though the conversation had never been interrupted: "Sometimes I feel like I have a really hard time being around Phoebe."

This was so direct, Grace couldn't see how to avoid it. So she asked, dutifully, "In what way?"

"Well, sometimes it seems like she's really mean to Gabriel."

She looked to Grace for encouragement, but Grace kept her face impassive.

"Like, I feel like she really tries to take advantage of him, and it makes me really upset."

Grace suddenly felt her eyes growing hot and watery. "She's not trying to take advantage of him," she said. "She's just acting like a normal toddler."

"Yeah, yeah, you're right about that, I know. But like, this feeling isn't really rational. You know? Like I know it's really screwed up to feel like you hate an eighteen-month-old girl. But just sometimes I feel like I can't stand to be in the same room with her."

Grace felt the tears begin to leak down her cheeks in hot, wet drops.

"Oh, God," said Angie. "I didn't mean to upset you. I mean, it's not like I hate *you*. I mean, I don't even hate her, I'm just being crazy. I'm sure it's not normal to feel this way. It's just, when she picks on Gabriel, and he gets upset and starts crying, it makes me feel like *I'm* upset, and *I* want to start crying."

"Well, of course," said Grace, making an effort to keep her voice from cracking. "Because mothers really identify with their kids. Because you can't separate your own needs from their needs, or your feelings from their feelings. So how do you think I can listen to what you're saying about Phoebe and not interpret it as a rejection of me?"

"Oh, Grace, but that's not what I meant at all," Angie said. "Oh, God, I really messed this up. I really like you. You're the best friend I have. I don't want to stop seeing you. But I was thinking, maybe we could just go out at night, when the kids are in bed. You know, dinners and movies. It's easier to talk then, anyway."

Now Grace was really crying, unable to stop herself. "Well, what am I supposed to tell Phoebe? She really likes Gabriel. You know, she really likes *you*."

Angie hid her face in her hands. "I'm just so sorry, Grace. It's not that I don't like her, don't you see? It's not really *about* her, it's about me."

Grace recognized the moment: This was the part of the date where the guy says, "It's not about you, it's about me. It's just that I need my space." And there was nothing you could say after that that would make any difference. Because it *was* about you, and the damage was already done.

◈

They slept in separate rooms that night. Sunday morning, over breakfast, they were elaborately cordial, and then they packed up the car and made strained small talk during the three-hour drive back.

Grace kept thinking of all the conversations they had had about discipline. The irony was, the friendship with Angie meant so much to her that she would have been willing to do practically anything Angie suggested to discipline Phoebe. And part of that was that the friendship, for Grace, was deeply based on this sense of shared values about things like discipline. But maybe all those times Angie had stood passively by watching Grace try to coax the kids past their conflicts, she had really been thinking to herself, "Why don't you *punish* her? Why don't you *yell* at her, so she'll learn to leave my precious Gabriel alone?" Maybe Angie had been lying about her feelings all along—even to herself—nurturing a secret resentment until it curdled into something so poisonous that Grace knew she would never again feel that she could fully trust Angie. The mosquito had stung.

But if she lost Angie completely, she'd have nothing, only that unbearable loneliness she had so recently, so gratefully, escaped. If she lost Angie, she'd go back to being the Alternative Weirdo woman in the Tot Lot, or she might even lose the Tot Lot altogether, because it would be awkward to snub or feud with someone you were bound to see every day, especially when your oblivious kids were likely to go on playing together anyway. And if she lost Angie, she'd lose the playgroup, because Grace's bond with Nina wasn't as strong as Angie's, so Grace would be the one who would have to drop out. And if she lost Angie, the Tot Lot, and the playgroup, she'd lose all the adhesive that currently bound her to society in her role as a Mother; her role as a Theater Person had already fully evaporated.

So there was nothing much to be done, after dropping Angie off at her apartment, other than to cling to the lifelines she had, being cool to Angie when she called (which she suddenly virtually stopped doing), and licking her wounds, as usual, in private.

Chapter 5

CAREER STORY
NINA

Women's lives offer valuable models because of the very pressures that make them seem more difficult. Women have not been permitted to focus on single goals but have tended to live with ambiguity and multiplicity. It's not easy. But the rejection of ambiguity may be a rejection of the complexity of the real world in favor of some dangerously simple competitive model.

Mary Catherine Bateson, Composing a Life

The new managerial mother sees her children as an addition to her life, not as a signal to switch her full attention from career to home. As *Working Woman*'s "Career Turning Points" survey pointed out just two months ago, having children (even three or more) doesn't hold career women back—professionally or financially.

Phyllis Schneider, "The Managerial Mother," in Working Woman *magazine, December 1987*

■ ■ ■

I spent the first two months of Sam's life cross-legged on the bed with a stack of fat pillows piled up on each knee. At any given moment, Sam would be on one or the other stack, latched ferociously onto one or the other breast, his little jaw working relentlessly to squeeze out every last possible drop of the Substance of Life Itself, while I paged just as relentlessly through yet another child-care book or parenting magazine, which I rested on the opposite stack of pillows, searching desperately for the currency that would allow me to redeem the rights to my apparently forfeited Life Story. Every twenty minutes or so I would switch breasts, and then after another twenty minutes I would hoist Sam onto my shoulder and pat pat pat his back until he belched like Falstaff, ejected a stream of the Substance of Life Itself down my back, and began to wail. Then I, too, would begin to wail, hurling the book or magazine across the room in frustration, and I would pull myself to my feet, and begin the long and ultimately fruitless process of trying to calm the baby down.

There is no question in the managerial mother's mind that she will return to work after her child is born. In fact, most are hesitant to be away for very long and may take a shorter than usual maternity leave.

There was no question in my mind that I was going to return to work as soon as possible. The question was: What did I have to return to? There was nothing, as far as I could tell, that I was on leave *from*, unless it was the basic core of my twenty-six-year-old identity as a competent, in-control, overachieving performer of logical verbal tasks. But if I went back to that, in the gung ho fifty-hour-a-week way that the Superwoman articles suggested I would naturally want to, then wouldn't I simply be on leave from the other, more fragile, newly born shoot of my core identity: the person who wanted to provide my miraculous infant with the moral, emotional, social, and intellectual—as well as physical— Substance of Life Itself; the reservoir in me that had been filling up for all those years purely in order to be drained? But then, if I allowed myself to be continually and unendingly drained, as the Earth Mother books and magazines suggested was the natural maternal state, by what means would I ever be replenished?

Ellis did not appear to be troubled by such considerations;

he was, in fact, not quite capable of disguising his relief as he apologetically backed out the door to go to work each morning. Leaving me to nurse and pace, nurse and pace, running the circular question of getting back to work in its endless paradoxical loop inside my head, like the endless paradoxical loop of the Substance of Life Itself that ran from my breasts into my child's mouth and was transmuted into his flesh, as well as into the stream of yellow spit-up down my back, and into the inconsolable pain and wailing that went on every night from dusk until dawn.

◈

At five o'clock every afternoon, I would allow myself to have a beer (not one minute earlier, or I might start to lose it)—my big treat: to feel pleasantly fuzzy, as the screaming began to escalate and I began to count the minutes until Ellis would walk in the door at six (not one minute later, or I would start to lose it). At the sound of his key in the lock, I would run to the front door, throw Sam into his arms, and race into the kitchen to cook dinner. Usually, the changing of the guard seemed to distract Sam into relative calm long enough for me to actually set dinner on the table. Then Ellis would deposit Sam into his baby bouncer, and Ellis and I would sit down at the table and hopefully begin a conversation, and then, within a bite or two, Sam's face would contort into a mask of tragedy and he would begin to howl.

I would slam down my fork and glare at Ellis. "It's been like this all fucking day. I can't stand it anymore. *You* take him for once." And I would stalk out.

Managerial mothers are challenging the long-held belief that child-rearing is the mother's responsibility by delegating considerable domestic duties to their husbands. . . . [The husbands] don't merely "pitch in" or "help out"; they are true partners.

Ellis (half an hour later, appearing tentatively in the doorway of the bedroom, where I am lying across the bed, leafing through yet another parenting publication): "I think he's hungry. He keeps sucking at my finger. Why don't you try nursing him?"

Me (half an hour later): "He's nursed. Listen, I've had him all day. You take him. Play with him or something."

(Ellis lies down on the couch, zooms Sam above his head like an airplane. Sam screams louder and spits up onto Ellis's head. Phone rings.)

Ellis: "Neen, it's for me. Can you come get Sam and take him in the other room?"

Me (half an hour later): "Ellis, I've had him *all day*. TAKE HIM!!"

(By nine-thirty or ten, Ellis gets Sam soothed to sleep and places him gently in the bassinet, then we both collapse into bed. At midnight Sam wakes, screaming. I get up and nurse him back to sleep, then lie awake anticipating the next interruption. I am still awake two hours later, when he screams again.)

Me (elbowing Ellis): "I've already been up with him once."

Ellis (groaning): "I've got to work tomorrow."

Me: "You mean today. And I've got to deal with him screaming all day."

(Ellis gives him a bottle, stays up with him for an hour, then wakes me up at three-thirty to take over. I stay awake with him for another hour or two, until miraculously his purple face and clenched fists gradually relax, and he slips off into sleep. I am so far beyond the edge of exhaustion, I no longer feel tired. But I must at some point drift off, because later I wake up again to the sound of wailing. The room is filled with sunlight. It is 8:15 A.M., and Ellis has already left for work.)

◈

All right, it is clear: I cannot go on day after day like this. I must return to my "I"—my Paper Self—as soon as possible. I must start writing about something. The byline under every single parenting magazine story reads, "So-and-So is a freelance writer who lives in ——— with her two small/teenage/grown children." So the logical thing to write about must be this motherhood business. My year in journalism school taught me how to structure stories like these—stories I might even be able to use to help solve my personal dilemmas. Take, for example, "How to Stop Your Baby from Crying." You open with a personal anecdote from a parent who formerly had this problem, cite the extent of the problem nationally using probably arbitrary statistics obtained from a Washington, D.C., or New York City institute, then explain how the parent solved the problem with the advice of Dr. So-and-So, a prominent crying expert on staff at a Very Important Hospital, and also, incidentally, author of a widely distributed paperback book on the subject. Now you need a few quotes from the great Dr. So-and-So himself, which gives you an excuse to call him up and slip in a couple of questions that are directly related to your particular situation, which you present as entirely hypothetical. You wrap up with the story of another parent whose crying-baby problems have been solved forever (not you, though; if you mention yourself in the story you are not being Objective. You are being Confessional. Journalists refer to Objective stories as "hard"— like those lean breastless hipless thighless boy/girl-bodies in the pages of the women's magazines—and to Confessional stories as "soft"—femininity unpruned, like the Chinese foot before the removal of the excess unaesthetic flesh. The desirability of one versus the other is supposed to be self-evident). Finally, you include material for a box the magazine will print against a pale blue or pink background listing six tips (from the esteemed Doctor's paperback) guaranteed to stop anyone's baby from crying.

The only trouble with my working on an article like this is that I have already read every single existing book on "How to Stop Your Baby from Crying" cover to cover at least twice, and have never found a single suggestion that worked with my child for more than five minutes at a time. Come to think of it, neither "How to Argue with Your Man—Constructively," nor "Making Those Postpartum Pounds Just Melt Away," nor "Finding Time in Your Busy Schedule—For YOU," each with their pastel boxed-and-numbered tips, has ever made the slightest practical dent in my Real Life. In fact, every time I even start to compare what the magazine experts insist my life is, could be, or should be about, I sense the ghost of my teenage self comparing my body to the cosmetically enhanced sylphs in *Seventeen;* and then I must try very consciously to convince myself that I am something other than a rogue elephant among women.

When Matthew was born, his parents' answer to the child care question was to hire a live-in au pair as well as a housekeeper who worked three days a week. Later the Sherwoods replaced the au pair with a governess. They decided that because the care-giver "would spend so much time with the boys, it was important to have someone who treated the job as a profession," says Sherwood. The governess . . . works Monday to Friday from 7:45 A.M. to 7 P.M. . . . . For the past year and a half a daily housekeeper has been taking care of the cleaning, laundry, shopping and cooking for Sherwood and her husband.

When an idea for a book began to take shape in the murk of my severely sleep-deprived mind, my answer to the child-care question was to take Sam two afternoons a week a few blocks away to the apartment of a Chinese graduate student and his wife who answered a classified ad I had placed in the local newspaper. They had neither experience nor references, but they did have a daughter six months older than Sam who had also screamed through her entire early infancy, and the wife gravely confided to me that babies who start out like that in life "are much smarter than those quiet ones." This remark, together with the clear child-centeredness of the small apartment, as well as some very fragrant and soothing green tea they served me on my first visit, convinced me to take a chance, even though at five dollars per hour, three hours per afternoon, the total weekly cost of thirty dollars was going to severely strain our budget. I was going to have to work fast.

My journalism training, still very fresh in my mind, inclined me toward something Hard. A practical book of facts, for example; how about a complete reference guide to resources available for Chicago parents, including hospitals, childbirth classes, and secondhand maternity boutiques? My elite liberal arts Yale education, on the other hand, inclined me toward something even Harder: a sociologically and politically important book of facts, such as an exhaustive and trenchant analysis of government and corporate attitudes toward the childbearing woman. But the sheaf of papers I sat down to every time Sam went to the baby-sitter's apartment took on an independent and rebellious life of its own. What began to obsess me was the way Motherhood didn't seem to me to have anything to do with the facts. Be Objective about Motherhood and you missed the whole story. Motherhood was by nature Soft. You couldn't even describe it in the language of facts and statistics I had been educated to speak and to believe was the only language in which any subject could be taken seriously in public discourse. The language of Mother-hood was a primitive language (my native language, now al-most completely lost) of joy and sadness and frustration and flesh and body processes and female gossip.

Unless the problem was me. Unless the values of Yale and journalism school and the parenting magazines, where every-thing was so Objective and Under Control and essentially Hard, were the true correct values, and I had simply faked my way into a set of impressive credentials of which I was not worthy. I felt I had to find out. So I spent a lot of that first year of limited working time in the kitchens and living rooms of other new mothers, tape-recording their feelings, trying to capture this other, elusive kind of truth. I couldn't ever shake the feeling that I was going about this essentially wrong, a feeling which, after I met Angie, I learned to identify as the Judy Chicago feeling: the sense that you are trying to express blood and womanhood in needlework, when in your heart you believe all They really want to see out there is naked succu-lent pink feminine flesh in oils.

◈

As for the housekeeping duties, Sam and I handled those to-gether on our days off, which, after we moved from Chicago to Westerville in the spring of 1988, were usually organized according to the ebb and flow of activity in the Tot Lot across the street, which in turn obeyed the ebb and flow of chil-dren's biorhythms and the programming schedule of the local PBS affiliate. There was rarely anyone in the Tot Lot until the second showing of *Sesame Street* ended at ten, but Sam woke up between six and six-thirty, so he usually got to watch both showings plus a Raffi tape because he lost interest in the tele-vision as soon as he heard the first notes of "It's a Beautiful

Day in the Neighborhood" (and informed me, the moment he learned to talk, "I doesn't like Rogers").

I would use this time to make coffee, feed myself and Sam, pack Ellis an economical lunch, take a shower, get dressed, clean up the kitchen, make our bed (there never seemed to be any point in making Sam's), and do whatever vacuuming or floor-scrubbing could no longer decently be delayed. At some point during the morning, usually while I had Comet all over my hands and the second *Sesame Street* was just ending, I would get a phone call from an editor or a source about some small freelance project I was doing. (I made calls only on the days when I had baby-sitting, but people called me back only on days when I didn't.) So then I would attempt to do a quick phone interview, trying to sound professional while Sam grabbed the phone cord, because he had recently got the impression that we thought it was extremely adorable for him to talk to people on the phone, or else he would be ominously quiet during the conversation and I would come back out to the living room afterward to find him sitting sheepishly next to a disaster that had occurred because I had taken off his diaper just before the phone rang and had not had a chance to replace it.

So then there would be more cleaning up, and chasing Sam around to get the new diaper and some clothes on him, which would mean dumping out the baskets of clean laundry that would have been sitting around for several days (after spend-ing several days in the dryer, after spending several days in the washer, because the facilities were in the basement of the building, where I refused to go since women were occasionally raped in the laundry rooms of neighborhood buildings; and Ellis's attitude toward laundry was somewhat casual). Sam would take this as his cue to demonstrate the juggling skills he had been practicing ever since seeing the Ringling Bros. and Barnum & Bailey Circus, which meant I had to make circus music while he stood at the foot of his bed, announced dramatically, "Ladies and gemmun," and hurled an armful of laundry into the air. Eventually he would start to throw the clothes at me and I would throw them at him, until finally one of us glanced out the window and noticed Phoebe or Gabriel in the Tot Lot. Then I would have an hour or two of simultaneous disjointed conversations with various mothers who were constantly being pulled away by children who wanted to be pushed or chased or caught or had gotten into a fight with other children or were climbing on something above a safe altitude.

Then it was lunchtime, which involved four or five warnings to the child that a departure was imminent (Gabriel learned, almost as soon as he could talk, to look at his wrist and tell Angie: "Five more minutes"). After the final warning, the child would throw him- or herself, screaming, to the ground, and refuse to leave, and so there would be a little procession of mothers and sitters issuing from the Tot Lot dragging flailing toddlers along with them.

Then there was making lunch, eating lunch, picking the remnants of lunch off the floor, and putting the child down for a nap. Then there was an hour and a half or so of Time to Myself, of which I typically wasted the first forty-five minutes trying to decide whether to read a book or read the paper or call a friend or transcribe a tape or clean the mold out of the refrigerator or switch the spring clothes to the front of the closet or take a nap or write a letter or write in my journal— because, after all, this was my only, very valuable, irreplaceable Time to Myself and I didn't want to waste it doing the wrong thing.

After Sam woke up, between two and three, we might go back to the Tot Lot or to the beach, or, as winter closed in, to Angie's apartment, or, more frequently, to do errands. But errands were always traumatic for both of us, because going into almost any store entailed confronting a large number of things each of us wanted and wasn't likely to get: for Sam, the endless succession of Teenage Mutant Ninja Turtle cookies, cereals, and snacks displayed throughout the supermarket, the Ghostbuster paraphernalia throughout Toys "R" Us, where we went to buy cheap diapers; for me, the interesting books I wouldn't have time to read, the elegant clothes I had no place to wear, the velvety plush towels that would get stolen from the laundry room—none of which Sam would let me drool over for long, always having an agenda of his own in every store, which was just as well, since we couldn't afford any of it, anyway.

By five o'clock, my head would be buzzing with amputated thoughts and conversation fragments, with yelled, unheeded "nos" and strangled longings, and my back would ache with the strain of innumerable boosts into and out of car seats and swings. Then I would turn on the news, pour myself a glass of red wine, and cook dinner.

Cooking dinner was for me a sacred ritual. I had done it for myself even when I lived alone, and I remembered my father doing it for my family as he drank his gin and tonic. It was not a domestic duty, it was a way of unwinding, a little trip into the sensually satisfying, uncomplicated world of aroma and taste, a project that could be started, finished, and consumed with simple pleasure. And while I concocted beef stews or pot roasts or stir fries or homemade spaghetti sauce, Sam would methodically unload all the drawers and cabinets below counter level, strewing cookie pans and rolling pins and egg-beaters across the floor, beating on pots with wooden spoons, clinging to my legs as I moved from sink to stove, commanding me to come play with him.

[Managerial couples] go to great lengths to spend as much time as possible with their children. "When we walk through the door at 6, we literally drop our briefcases and start playing with the girls," says Priscilla. "We don't even bother to change clothes. At 7:30 I bathe the children and get them ready for bed."

Ellis would walk through the door sometime around six, and I would be mad at him because he was late and dinner had burned or cooled off, or because he didn't immediately peel Sam off my legs, or just because I had had a long and frustrating day and he had gone to a quiet office where I supposed he was left alone to think in peace. And he would be in a bad mood because he had gotten stuck on the packed El train or because he had walked in to find me mad at him.

And so the civilized dinner conversation at the rickety teak card table would eventually degenerate into an argument over whose turn it was to clean up the kitchen and whose it was to perform the still-daunting task of coaxing Sam into the mood to sleep. And this might in turn lead us into even more dangerous territory: an argument over which of us worked harder, the one who'd spent the day Working, or the one who Hadn't.

◆

In January of 1989, after I had calmed down about Angie and returned, slightly defensively, to the playgroup, I began to notice that my body was up to something. At ten-thirty one unseasonably warm Saturday morning, as Ellis was driving Sam and me to the Lincoln Park Zoo, my blood sugar suddenly dropped so low I was positive I was going to pass out unless Ellis pulled over instantly and bought me a hot dog (I don't normally like hot dogs). A few days later, moments after I had left the apartment with Sam in his stroller, I had to make a U-turn and rush frantically back to pee. It was another week be-

fore I even missed the first period; but unlike my first pregnancy, so strange and upsetting to me physically—a really bad
scene from *Invasion of the Body Snatchers*—this time I recognized the territory, and accepted the signals for what they
were.

I suppose it seems odd that I would allow myself this second pregnancy, after all the stress and career compromise and
marital strain and sheer boredom and frustration of the first
experience—still clearly unresolved. I can only attempt to explain it this way:

One day that March, just as I was emerging from the fog of
my morning sickness, and just as Sam was turning two, we
were driving home from the gymnastics class I'd signed him
up for because of his enduring obsession with the circus and
with acrobats. Sam reached for the steering wheel and demanded, "I drive."

"No, Sam," I said. "Only grown-ups drive."

"*I* drive," Sam repeated, more insistently.

I braced for the inevitable fight: "No, you can't," "I WANT
TO," "No, you can't," "I WANT TO." I was tired and distracted and not in the mood to have the argument, so I simply began to chatter above his conversational level, hoping to
bore him to distraction.

"In America, Sam, we have laws. Laws are like rules you
have in your house, only everyone in the whole country has
to follow laws. And in America we have a law that says you
have to be sixteen years old to drive a car. You're two. So you
need to wait fourteen more years before you can drive. See?"

He was quiet for a few moments, which I took as a promising sign that he had lost interest. But then he reached one
chubby little leg over, kicked the car door, and said,
"Awwwwwww. I doesn't *like* America."

That was what my body had made; *that* was what my milk
had made; *that* was what my sensibility had made (the Sub-

stance of Life Itself): a gorgeous independent human, who is you and yet is not. This romance between you and your child, it is as blind and as physically compelling as any bond with a lover. But with a lover, as the physical connection begins to wane, the whole relationship may lose its allure; whereas with a child, as the physical connection wanes, the sheer fact that a complete separate person is left standing there, becoming more and more Himself with every passing day, creates a seduction ongoing, on levels ever deeper and more compelling.

◈

"So you weren't satisfied by the way your first labor was handled," said Dr. Mary Appleton. Unwilling to return to the obstetrician who had handled my first nightmarish birth, I had picked her out of a list provided by a physician referral service. She was a woman, so I assumed she would understand.

"It was very, very painful," I said. But as soon as I said it, I knew that wasn't the thing I was dissatisfied about, exactly. I was dissatisfied because I felt I had danced ignited through the flames of hell and the doctor hadn't been there and the staff had merely acted like this was barely notable. But I could already tell it wouldn't do much good to explain this to Dr. Appleton, who was young and cheerful and, as it turned out, herself child-free.

"Well, usually we find that second labors are shorter and quite a bit easier than first labors," she said.

"Yes, but even so, I had this feeling of being, I don't know, *abandoned* to the pain."

Dr. Appleton checked something in her notes and looked at me quizzically. "But you say you were given Dilaudid."

"Yes. But it didn't seem to be very effective in stopping the pain."

"I see," said Dr. Appleton. "Well, maybe it's time for us to think about an epidural. But we can talk about that closer to your due date. Did you have any other questions?"

◆

"So why did that bother you?" Angie asked after I described the exchange at the next playgroup meeting.

"Because I just have a feeling I don't *want* an epidural. It just sounds like, I don't know, such a Managerial Mother kind of thing. Like: 'Let's use the most modern and efficient methods and keep you quiet and happy so that I, the busy physician, can deliver three other babies simultaneously and optimize customer satisfaction and the hospital's cost structure at the same time!'"

Out of the corner of my eye, I thought I saw Grace smirking. But it might have been just my imagination. It was me, not Grace, who was the smirking type.

"Then what *do* you want?"

"I want someone to sit next to me the whole time and hold my hand."

"Won't Ellis sit next to you and hold your hand?" asked Grace.

"Yeah. But it's not the same thing. He was just as scared as I was, because he didn't have any idea what was going on, and he didn't have any authority to make decisions. I want the *doctor* to sit next to me and hold my hand."

"Then what you want," said Grace, "is a midwife."

That was such a Grace answer. Grace had already decided that not only did she intend to try to have her next baby at home—despite having had the emergency C-section the first time—but she planned to let Phoebe watch the whole thing. Of course, it made sense in the context of her holistic-vege-

tarian-homeopathic, environmentally aware, politically correct life. But to me it sounded excessively Alternative. It is
one thing to make Rogue Elephant decisions on your own be-
half, but where your children are concerned, you want to have
150 years of the Male Medical Establishment on your side.

"The human race did manage to reproduce for tens of
thousand of years before the male medical establishment
came along," Grace pointed out, "and still manages to over-
populate sections of the planet."

"You can have *both*," said Angie. Her HMO had used
nurse-midwives, practicing under the supervision of an obstetrician, who delivered at Westerville Hospital. She recalled
now that the doctor, who was a woman, had since gone into
private practice and was working with two new nurse-midwives, and she gave me the name.

"Our mothers would definitely freak out," Ellis said, when I
tried the idea out on him, by which I understood him to
mean: "*I* am really freaked out."

But as the days went by, I realized I had no desire to go
back and see the safely and scientifically professional Dr. Appleton. I gave the midwife a call.

◈

Leonora, who invited me to call her by her first name, *looked*
like a midwife. Her waist-length, light brown hair, worn loose
over her white medical jacket, gave her an air of eighteenth-
century witchiness that immediately appealed to me. She
wore no makeup; her eyes were brown and steady, and her
bearing was rather grave.

As we sat in Leonora's office, I told her the story of Sam's
birth, then told her about telling it to Dr. Appleton, and

what Appleton had replied about the epidural. When I finished, I held my breath and waited to see whether Leonora would get it.

Leonora regarded me for a long moment, blinking once or twice, and then said carefully, "One of the main advantages a midwife has to offer is that she is present throughout the birth. So we can work with you in ways that an obstetrician normally would not. One of the things I would want to do between now and your due date is to try to determine what techniques might work best for you in labor—breathing, visualization, massage, hot showers or baths. I'm not saying you can't use medication if you want to use it, but there are plenty of strategies that we can try before we go to that."

Then she explained what she saw as my risks: She and the other midwife almost always delivered their own patients, but if for some reason she was unavailable, or if the labor ran into complications, there was always some chance that either the other midwife or the doctor would deliver me. But those were the only two possibilities, and she would make sure I had appointments with both of them well before the due date so that I would know them.

And, she said, the doctor would be taking over in October as chief of obstetrics in a small nearby hospital that I knew did not have the reputation or the high-tech facilities of Westerville Hospital. And since my due date was early in October, I could expect to be one of the first of their patients to deliver there.

"Our mothers *really* aren't going to like *that*," Ellis said.

I went to see the little hospital. Its maternity floor was newly renovated, the rooms converted to LDRPs, meaning I would labor, deliver, recover, and spend my postpartum days all in the same room. The rooms looked like hotel-chain suites. The walls were papered in mauve; two-thirds of the room had highly polished light-wood flooring, and at the far end was a gray-carpeted sitting area, with a gray-and-mauve couch, two easy chairs, a round wooden table, and a big light-wood cabinet that proved to contain a TV set. The bed was in the floored area, where there was also a sink and some cabinets, but most of the medical equipment was cleverly hidden behind innocuous-looking panels. Each room had a neat private bathroom with a small Jacuzzi.

I remembered Westerville Hospital: being wheeled through the halls on a gurney when I was screaming and thrashing and totally out of control; the roommate who chattered incessantly into the phone (after she finally gave up trying to engage me in conversation); the tiny shared bathroom, with a shower stall that had evidently been designed for a space capsule.

This was certainly nicer. But queerly empty. Of the twelve rooms, only two were currently occupied. At Westerville they parked women in the halls until rooms became available. Was there something really horrible about this hospital that I didn't know?

This might be a good time to contact a parenting magazine about the possibility of writing an article: "Midwife Births— Are They *Really* Safe?" But I could already write the whole article in my head: the spokesperson from the American College of Obstetricians and Gynecologists, who would assert that only obstetricians have been fully educated to properly manage the full range of potentially serious complications of birth, versus the representative from the national midwives' association, who would insist that birth is essentially a Natural, not a Medical, event. I could take it like a Man ("and more of a man each day")—grin and bear it and control myself at all costs; or I could take it like a Woman—an Earth Mother or a Radical Feminist, surrendering to the Goddess drug free; or I could simply have someone sit there and hold my hand while I tried to get through whatever came, taking it like the Rogue Elephant Among Women I truly am.

In the end Leonora's calm brown eyes won me over. I decided to trust her, and, if possible, to try to trust myself. And I made a mental note that when I talked to my mother and mother-in-law about this, I must remember to be vague.

At Grace's in late January, Angie casually announced that she had met a woman she really liked in the Tot Lot and had invited her to join the group.

Grace and I looked at each other in alarm.

"She's new here," Angie explained. "She lives in England, and she's only gonna be here for eight months while her husband does some kind of fellowship at Westerville, and I felt sorry for her. Who's she gonna meet in the Tot Lot in the middle of winter?"

"Well, she met you," I pointed out. "And you're saying you don't even *know* her? You just kind of *picked her up?*"

Angie shrugged. "I didn't think about it. It didn't occur to me you guys would get so upset."

"We're not upset," Grace said, in that same strenuously even voice she used when she was pointedly *not* yelling at Phoebe. "I think our concern, Angie, is that over the course of the past four months, we've developed a lot of intimacy and trust here. And with a stranger, we might not feel as free to discuss a lot of the kinds of things we like to talk about."

"But she'll fit right in," Angie said, entreatingly. "She's real, real smart, she reads a lot, and it seems like she's kinda mad at her husband."

Grace and I exchanged another look. We weren't close enough ever to have talked about Angie together behind her back, so neither of us was aware of the recent breach in the other's friendship. But I think we were both feeling at that point that the playgroup had actually become encumbered by its intimacy and undermined in terms of trust. Upsetting the balance would not necessarily be a bad thing. And anyway, it appeared to be a fait accompli.

◙

Margaret looked like a person who wanted not to be noticed, and Grace and I were both fascinated by her instantly. She dressed unstylishly, in old jeans and worn, drab men's shirts that camouflaged her body. Her hair was very short, appearing to have been chopped off rather than cut, possibly by herself, and it was hard to get a sense of what her face looked like behind her very large, exceedingly thick glasses.

She was unconditionally committed to the needs of her family. Her husband, Ron, was a kind of itinerant scholar, wandering from appointment to fellowship around the globe according to the offers that came in, monkishly absorbed in his work, which he pursued six-and-a-half days a week (he came home early on Saturdays so Margaret could take a dance class).

Margaret simply followed him, apparently oblivious to her surroundings. Their Westerville sublet was horrifically ugly, filled with decades-old yellow shag carpeting, hysterically busy brown-and-gold wallpaper, and green vinyl furniture, none of which Margaret seemed to notice. She concentrated all of her energy and attention on her fragile and astoundingly precocious two-year-old daughter, Jane, who ignored the still largely preverbal tantrums of the other playgroup children while she played elaborate make-believe games with their toys, explaining to you in her crisp British enunciation, if you inquired, about birds who were singing in the "hedges" or a documentary she had recently viewed on PBS "concerning animation."

Margaret was not full of conflict about her life. She explained this by pointing out that she was ten years older than the rest of us, and had had the sixties and the chance to get drugs and wild oats and a decidedly uncompelling career as a librarian out of her system before having children. She made wry references to Ron's domestic elusiveness, but when the rest of us really got going about our husbands, she would shrug and say, "I knew he was like that when I married him. It was one of the things that I loved about him, his commitment to his work."

Grace was captivated by the purity of her performance as a mother. All the things Grace thought it would be Good and Stimulating to do all day with Phoebe, but rarely had the patience to sustain, Margaret actually did all day with Jane. There was homemade play dough and little art projects made out of cereal boxes and toothpicks and hours and hours of make-believe in which Jane made up the scenarios and Margaret patiently held up her end of the dialogue. The relationship between Margaret and Jane seemed utterly mature. You never, ever saw Jane misbehave, and on the rare occasions when another child hurt her and she began to wail, you were shocked to remember that she wasn't a miniature adult after all, but only two years old; and there was no hint that Margaret actually had a temper, let alone ever lost it.

Since Margaret had no work commitments, no local friends, and no car, Grace took it upon herself to show her around, organizing little trips to the children's museum or the aquarium. Soon, they were seeing each other almost daily, and the friendship very neatly filled the hole that had been left in Grace's life by her rift with Angie. Grace felt that she was, in effect, understudying Margaret. How was it that Margaret could subordinate herself completely to the needs of her child and husband—yet not lose her sense of self? Were some people just like that—so warm and giving that they made the people around them feel wonderful, and derived from that the fulfillment that let them go on making people feel wonderful? But the feminism Grace had grown up with had preached that work, money, and independence were the only true sources of self; that in serving others, you became a servant—inferior, disposable, unsafe, unadmired. So Grace, being a feminist, was a little suspicious of Margaret's apparent contentment. But if the contentment was real, then maybe Margaret understood The Secret of Life.

I didn't see Margaret much outside of playgroup, but I was fascinated by what I knew of her past. In addition to having been a librarian, she had once worked in a bookstore; she had read everything I could think of in English and American literature, and evidently had taken it all seriously. And yet here she was, playing make-believe with a two-year-old, no regrets. And there was the photograph she would show you, with a mixture of pride and sheepishness, of herself in her early twenties, dancing: a delicate, lithe body balanced *en pointe* in sinewy grace; huge expressive eyes in a beautifully sculpted face, gazing romantically away from the camera, her long shiny hair done up in an elegant bun. And yet here she was: camouflaged, no regrets. Was it really possible that well-educated, modern women could just walk away from the young, yearning, striving parts of themselves and occupy themselves with make-believe and play dough for days on end? Was it possible they could renounce all worldly things—chop off their hair like a nun pledging herself to God, but pledging themselves instead to a family, no regrets? Knowing the strife that went on all day, every day, in my own soul, I doubted it. But if her renunciation was real, then maybe Margaret understood The Secret of Life.

Ironically, it was Angie who formed the least intimate bond with Margaret during the eight months Margaret was with us. But Angie liked her, liked something about her presence that was very calm and steady and quiet. Margaret never talked about herself much, so Angie never found out what it might

be, but Angie imagined there was some terrible tragedy em-
bedded in Margaret's past that gave her the quality Angie
sensed in her: the capacity to listen to another person's sadness, and empathize infinitely.

◈

"She's arguing that we all have to face the fact that women
workers really are *different* from men workers because women
have babies. So listen to this, and I quote: 'Without a strategy
for handling these women . . . companies pay a high price.
They don't get *a full return on their investment* in training
some women for top jobs if the women quit or are unable to
put in long hours after they become mothers.' Now could
someone please tell me what drives me crazy about that
logic?"

I was waving the current issue of *Newsweek* at the others,
gathered around the table in the Mexican restaurant, sipping
their Dos Equis, while I virtuously, in honor of my already ex-
panding belly, sipped ginger ale. Angie had gotten us all to
agree to what she called "Woman of the Full Moon" meetings
(the Efé Pygmies consider menstruation a blessing to be cele-
brated, and Pygmy women "usually menstruate together
around the time of the full moon"). The point was to leave
the fathers in charge of the children one evening a month so
we could all go out to a restaurant and celebrate ourselves.

"It seems to me," said Angie, "like one of those weird situations where politics meets reality and we end up having to
have a big public fight over which is which. Like these
women employees are saying, 'Hey, we *like* these babies;
they're cuter and more fun to be with than the marketing
manager for the new product line,' and then the feminists are
going to run in and say, 'SSSSSSSSSSSHHH! You can't say

that! It makes women look like wimps in the workplace.'"

"Feminists," said Grace, "are just trying to say you can't make the *assumption* that every woman is going to feel that way."

"*We* all feel that way," said Angie.

"No, we don't," I said. "I didn't lose interest in working because I had a baby. I just didn't want to be forced to choose *between* working and having the baby. I just didn't want some corporation telling me that I couldn't be a successful person unless I worked X number of hours at X location doing X job, whereas if I worked fewer hours doing some other kind of job, I would be consigned forever to some inferior 'Mommy Track' circle of mediocrity."

"What bothers me about this whole thing," said Margaret, "is the way they seem to assume everyone in this whole hypothetical corporation is performing like a dynamo, except the women having babies. Why don't they propose a separate track for men who get practically nothing done for a year or two while they go through a depression or a divorce or an affair or a mid-life crisis? Why do they just assume that men don't have any experiences outside the office that compromise peak performance?"

"Because they still assume," Grace said, "that any real life that happens to a man outside his workplace is going to be taken care of by his wife."

"So we haven't moved forward at all," I said. "We used to be sex objects and domestic objects, and now we're corporate objects; if they don't get a full return on their investment, they have to find a way to repackage us."

The waiter arrived with four enormous combination plates, throwing the conversation off while we strove to remember who had ordered what. Next to us, the hostess was seating a young couple with a baby that was perhaps a year old.

"Shit," said Angie. "I hope it's a quiet one. Why does that

always happen in a restaurant whenever you finally manage to get a night off from your own kid?"

"Speaking of sex objects," said Margaret, "who's been to see the new Disney film?"

"Gabriel would never sit through a movie," said Angie.

"I'd want to see it myself before taking Phoebe," said Grace. "I'm not sure she's psychologically ready for movies yet, and Disney films always have such stereotypical female characters."

"We saw it," I said. "And I didn't think it was that bad. The mermaid is gorgeous, of course, in a kind of Barbie doll way. And, of course, the point of it is for her to get the prince. But I don't know, she probably has more interesting and challenging adventures getting her prince than I had getting mine. Or doing any of my jobs, certainly."

"Let me guess," Angie said. "The prince is very strong and handsome, with big muscles."

"Yes," I conceded.

"And there's a benevolent father figure and an evil, destructive, witchy mother figure," said Margaret.

"Yes."

"And they must have cleaned up the plot," said Grace.

"What do you mean?"

"Well, in the original, she has her tongue cut out. And when her tail splits into legs, every step she takes feels as though she's walking on knives. It's like the original *Cinderella*, where the sisters cut their heels off to try to get into the glass slipper—which is supposed to derive historically from stories about Chinese foot binding. It's all this same tradition of women mutilating themselves to get a man."

I explained that in the Disney version, the mermaid just temporarily loses her voice.

"I have that feeling, sometimes," Margaret said quietly, "but it wasn't getting my man that gave it to me. It was having a child." She stopped, probably taken aback by the way we had all suddenly stopped eating, our utensils in the air, waiting to see what she would say next—something oracular, perhaps, which would finally reveal the secret of her contentment.

"I've been repackaged," she continued, "as a person outside the realm of public discourse. I'm not on the Mommy Track, or any track. It's not that I'm bored spending all the time with Jane that I do, or that I even regret having given up all those other things I used to do. It's just I feel sometimes that my voice is getting softer and softer, and someday I'll say something, and no one will be able to hear me at all."

She said it matter-of-factly, as though she really had been repackaged, as though her feelings were all safely contained within her motherly and wifely contentment. But I was thoroughly chilled. There it was, wasn't it? The one ineluctable fact about Motherhood, from which feminism had never managed to rescue us. Feminism had made it possible for us to live with men without chopping off bits of ourselves, of our will and our desire. But Motherhood still poses us all with that mermaid's choice: Have your children, stay home with them, and give up your voice in public discourse and the marketplace; or keep your voice, and sign the kids over to a caretaker who might turn out to be a witch. The marketplace demands total commitment; anything less and they automatically shove you in the corner with the Mommy Track dunce cap on; in the other corner are the child psychologists, insinuating that anything less than total commitment to child rearing will result in a permanently damaged child. So those of us who wish not to mutilate ourselves—not to let go of all will and desire, while still having and loving children—end up struggling through a great mine field of guilt and logistical and financial obstacles, until under the stress bits of us begin to crack and break off anyway.

The restaurant's strolling guitarist had stopped at the next table and was playing the *Sesame Street* theme song to the toddler, who was beaming and clapping and flirting in that shameless way especially beautiful babies have. Angie, Grace, and Margaret had all stopped talking and were watching the child, their faces lost in dreamy vicarious rapture, and after a moment I felt the same doting smile melt my own expression.

"A primitive reflex," I commented a few moments later, after the guitarist had begun wailing, "AYE-yae-yae-yae," and the toddler had begun whining and trying to squirm out of the high chair; after the spell had broken and we had all returned to our senses.

Because, after all, this was our night off.

CHAPTER 6

VOICE STORY

ANGIE

It is frightening when a woman finally realizes that there is no answer to the question 'who am I' except the voice inside herself.

Betty Friedan, The Feminine Mystique

■ ■ ■

Angie dangled between the two extremes of Grace and Nina, like the threads that dangled from the quilt she lacked the perseverance to complete. By now she had lost patience with the Grace approach to Motherhood; sometimes she got the feeling she didn't have enough Self for herself, let alone extra to spare endlessly indulging Gabriel's needs. Grace's approach still seemed ideal, but Nina's seemed more practical, more humane to the mother—you got something, the kid got something. But how Angie could ever get herself to a place like that seemed another draining task she just didn't have the energy to undertake.

Just doing laundry could consume whole days. The laundry room was in the basement across the alley. So to get to it, first Angie had to get Gabriel into his snowsuit and boots, which took half an hour because he hated going out and ran away or wrestled with her the whole time.

So she was already exhausted and pissed off as she maneuvered Gabriel and two baskets of laundry down the rickety back stairway, keeping an eye out for any creepy potential rapists hanging around. Then, while she was putting the laundry in the washer, Gabriel ran around the basement like a puppy suddenly let off the leash, and he was especially drawn to the filthy dark part where she suspected all the mousetraps and rat poison were hidden. Then she caught him again, towed him back through the alley and up the stairs, peeled off the boots and the snowsuit, and waited forty-five minutes for the wash cycle to be finished so she could go back down and put things in the dryer.

Sometimes Angie would drive out to her mother's little bungalow in the suburbs, where there was a washer and dryer right off the kitchen—not to mention an automatic dishwasher—and then later, when she was driving back to Westerville with Gabriel next to her in the beat-up Toyota, she'd just start crying. All that space and nice furniture and convenience, and her mom didn't even have kids to take care of anymore. And here she was, envying her mom, when she had sworn in high school she would rather die than grow up to be like her. It had seemed then that she was superior to, so much stronger than, her mom, so much smarter; she knew that women didn't have to spend their whole adult lives dependent on men. But now somehow she was just like a small child again, always calling up her mom to ask for help, even though she could still hear that voice in her head that she had struggled so hard against, her mom's voice, the voice that screamed "DON'T HAVE SEXUAL INTERCOURSE" and "DON'T JUMP ON THE FURNITURE" and "I MIGHT KILL MYSELF AT ANY MOMENT" with equal fervor. Angie tried so hard not to let that voice come out of her own mouth. She tried so hard to be gentle and to channel Gabriel's energy into something nondestructive, and her own energy into something creative, but sometimes he just got this totally wild out-of-control look like he was maybe about to trash the house, and then Angie would feel the scream starting to come out of her mouth and she didn't know what to do. Neither Nina nor

Grace seemed to have this problem, and why was it that things that were so easy for other people were so impossible for her?

And so this Earth Mother business didn't work out because you were just so pissed off at the kid all the time, and as for the Fiber Arts—yeah, right, like Gabriel was going to let her have a couple of hours of peace and quiet to get a project going. What would've made sense was a couple of days of day care, like Nina had. But when Angie mentioned this possibility to Jeff, he flipped.

"I thought when you decided you wanted this baby the whole point was for you to take care of it yourself. Babies aren't like dogs, Angie; you don't just give them away when you get tired of them."

But she kept after him, and after a while he conceded that it probably wouldn't be so terrible if, one or two mornings a week, Gabriel went to the house of a woman Angie knew from the Tot Lot. So, one day in February, Angie walked Gabriel over to the woman's house. She was going to get three hours of child care, but she spent at least the first half hour lingering at the woman's house over a cup of coffee, terrified of the actual moment of separation. Then she walked the few blocks home as sssslooowly as she could, but when she got there, there were still almost two whole hours of time to fill. She didn't like being alone in the apartment; it made her feel jittery, unanchored, abandoned. She couldn't remember why it had seemed so important for her to have this time to herself. Oh, she was going to design and sew Gabriel's summer wardrobe.

She turned on a Tracy Chapman tape and pulled out the box of fabrics she had been saving. She wasn't really in the mood to do kids' clothes. But there were some interesting scraps: a very deep, rich purple, and a gray and a mossy green she thought it would look good with. But it wasn't enough for a whole quilt, and she didn't have the patience for a quilt right now, not the tedious kind with the squares. She waited for some voice inside her to tell her what to do with the scraps.

Sometimes she just started with the picture in her head and a pair of shears in her hands, improvising totally from scratch. If the idea was strong, she could work for a long time like that, leaving the quilt out where she could see it even when she wasn't working, checking every day to see what it needed to have added or taken away or softened. And that would go along great, until one day she would look at it, and suddenly come out of her trance: It would look AWFUL. It would be unbearably dumb and humiliating and amateurish, like something a kindergartner would bring home. She would think, "What the *hell* was I doing?" and she might show it to a friend who stopped by, who would look at it politely, so that Angie could tell she was secretly thinking, "What the *hell* is she doing?" They always liked the pretty quilt, the one with the squares. The thing she could do if she was good, and followed all the rules. But when they saw the one with the real *her* put into it, they got disgusted, just like her mother and father and everyone had gotten disgusted with her after she hit adolescence and stopped following all the rules. And what was the point, then, of sending your child to the care of strangers—so you could rip yourself open and reveal everything hideous and humiliating within yourself?

And what if Jeff was right about day care? What if what she was really doing was sending Gabriel the terrible message that he wasn't wanted at home? That was the other way she had sworn not to be like her mom: her mom, sliding down against the wall; her mom, missing for weeks from the household; her mom, who was never, ever there for Angie, to help Angie through *her* pain, as now Angie wasn't there helping Gabriel through the pain of separation.

Angie checked her watch. There was still an hour and a

half left, but she just couldn't bear staying in the apartment alone any longer. The first day of day care was special, she decided. On the first day, it wouldn't seem too totally wimpy if she just showed up kind of on the early side to pick him up.

◈

That old weird feeling started coming over her again at night, that aching in the wrists, the throbbing sensation that invited her to slice, that promised slicing would be a release. Angie was getting scared. There was no logic to this feeling, no thought process, like: "Life is not worth living, therefore I will kill myself." There must be something chemical, something inherited from her mother, or something related to PMS. Because she was still pretty sure nothing was really wrong with her. And so she tried to ignore the feelings, and she got up every morning and went on.

◈

The summer days blurred together in her mind. Nina's belly blossomed under her uncharacteristically pink maternity jumper, and in late July, Grace returned from a month's vacation at the Michigan house with the news that she, too, was pregnant again. (That kind of creativity, too, exposed you, ultimately ripped your insides out, but revealed something sheerly wonderful for you and the world to marvel at. Unless you were married to Jeff, who regarded the process and its result with scorn and disgust; which was why Angie would not allow herself to become pregnant again.)

In less than a month, Margaret and Ron would be returning to England, and Angie and Grace decided to make her a small quilt as a souvenir. Angie would make two squares—her favorite shapes, the flower and the windmill—and Grace would also sew two: a pair of dancing legs, in honor of Margaret's ballet dancing, and a moon setting over the earth, to symbolize the Woman of the Full Moon dinners.

It was Angie who stitched the whole thing together, by hand. It look hours and hours, much longer than she had expected, but then, it had been so long since she had actually finished any of her projects. On the night before Margaret was leaving, Angie still had about three more hours of work to do, and Gabriel wouldn't leave her alone, and Jeff was doing his usual routine of promising to take care of him and then letting him drift into Angie's room "by accident." So finally Angie took all the fabric and the sewing supplies out to the Toyota parked in front of the apartment building and turned on the overhead lights and stitched furiously until the whole thing was done.

She was so proud of that quilt. It came out beautiful, and she could tell Grace and Nina honestly thought so, too, and she thought Margaret almost cried when she unwrapped it, although Margaret was too strong a person ever to cry.

◈

Jeff was beginning to drop serious hints about a transfer. He was at the stage, he said, where the company expected you to prove your loyalty by making a big move—in other words, by ripping up your community roots and overriding your wife's life and your kids' friendships, to establish, beyond a shadow of a doubt, that you took work SERIOUSLY—and they had better start thinking about what they could tolerate, so he could jump at the right opportunity when it came. The prospects he mentioned were all overwhelming to Angie: the

Philippines, Paris, Luxembourg, Connecticut. There was some block in her brain against even thinking about them; how could she possibly feel at home in any of these foreign places when she didn't even feel at home in her own skin? But what was she going to do? Leave Jeff and stand on her own two feet, with Gabriel to raise and support? When she could barely stand on her own two feet with Jeff propping her up? No, she had no alternative but to follow him.

But her wrists ached and throbbed, whispering, "This is a trap, and you are suffocating, and you have to claw your way out." She seized at the idea of Margaret's quilt, the only thing that had made her feel good in such a long time. The husband of her old quilting teacher had offered to rent her a room above their garage that she could use as a studio. She could put Gabriel in real day care two days a week, and go to the studio and work, and sell her quilts at the store in Westerville where she had taken lessons.

She went to look at the YMCA, where they had a flexible day-care program and you could sign up your kid for almost any combination of full or part days. She arranged it very carefully so that when she presented it to Jeff it would sound logical and sensible and businesslike, and he would not be able to twist it all around to make it sound like it had arisen out of her weakness.

But then, somehow, he did. He hated the idea of the Y, even more than he had hated the idea of the woman caregiver from the Tot Lot. This was institutional child care, he said. Gabriel was way too young; he'd get lost in a big class of kids. And how were they going to pay for it, until she started making enough money from the quilts to pay for it herself?

In the end, they compromised: She would take the studio, at very minimal rent, but she would only work there two evenings a week and on Saturdays, when Jeff could watch Gabriel.

But that went badly. At night, she was worn out from the long hours of amusing and containing and cleaning up after Gabriel, and all she really felt like doing was curling up in bed with a book or renting a videotape. On Saturdays, if the weather was bad, she left home preoccupied with the idea that Jeff was just going to let Gabriel sit in front of the television all day. If the weather was good, she would be distracted by her yearning for all the fun things they might be doing together as a family—which was all she had really wanted in the first place, anyway. It was just because Jeff resisted being a family that she was having to go out and build some other identity for herself.

And so mostly she sat in the studio and stared at fabric swatches and wondered, again, how Jeff could have changed so much from the loving, supportive man she had married. She didn't sew much of anything, except a couple of rag dolls, and they'd never sell, since they struck even Angie as looking kind of creepy.

◆

Late in September, Monique came to visit. She had long since moved back to France, but she was in Chicago for a few days on business, and one evening she took the train up to Westerville for dinner. Angie was excited; Monique was the one person who really seemed to like and understand her creative work. She showed Monique the doll she had just finished, with the big droopy breasts whose nipples pointed downward and the blue lace underpants.

"The lace doesn't look right; it doesn't belong there," Monique said, frowning.

"Yeah, it does," said Angie. "I can't say why, I just know it does."

"She looks bloated and sad, like a depressed housewife," said Monique, who looked chic and glowing, like a transatlantic jet-setting businesswoman. "She looks like you."

◆

"She *said* that?" asked Nina incredulously in the Tot Lot the next day. Nina was only about two weeks away from her due date now, and sat awkwardly at the edge of the sandbox, unable to bend all the way over the bulge of her stomach. "And you didn't kick her out of your house?"

"Well, she wasn't trying to be mean," said Angie. "She's just one of those really blunt people who says exactly what she thinks. She's real strong that way."

"Well, I'd rather not have people like that as friends," said Nina, which only made Angie feel worse, because now, in addition to kicking herself over Monique's insult, she would kick herself for having handled it wrong. Why was everything like that these days, fuck-ups leading to worse fuck-ups?

"So listen," Angie said, to change the subject. "I just found out, Jeff is going to Atlanta for three days next week, so if you go into labor then, I might have some trouble taking care of Sam."

"That's okay," Nina said. "We've got some backup people lined up. And besides, I don't think I'm the type who delivers early."

◆

Angie decided to cope resourcefully with Jeff's trip to Atlanta, even though every time she thought of it a wave of panic shot through her body. So the next Monday, the day he was scheduled to leave, she packed Gabriel into the Toyota, along with a picnic lunch, and drove him to a park she'd never explored before.

It was the second of October, and fall had swallowed Indian summer some time in the middle of the previous night. As soon as they got to the park, it was clear that the whole picnic idea had been stupid. The cold, sharp wind cut like a scalpel through the flimsy sweatshirt and light jacket Angie was wearing. The clouds were thick and fat and gray and low, and some of the trees had already lost all of their leaves and looked stark and black against the sky. Another Chicago winter on the way; another six months cooped up inside, alone. How could she possibly live through it?

She chased Gabriel a little bit, hoping to warm herself up, then pushed him on the swing. She could smell that his diaper needed changing, and she felt like she'd had it with the cold.

"Gabriel," she said, "come on, we're leaving."

"No!" he shouted, and ran in the opposite direction.

Angie took a deep breath. "Okay," she called. "But just five more minutes."

But when she called him again, he dived into a clump of bushes.

"I mean it, Gabriel," she said, standing right outside the shrubs. "Come out before I count to five. One . . . two . . . three . . ."

"I'm not comin' out," Gabriel sang merrily.

She didn't have the patience for this. She lunged into the mass of prickly branches and felt around until she caught an arm, and then she dragged him out.

"OWWW, that HURTS," he shrieked.

She heaved him up onto her hip and began striding toward the car. Gabriel screamed and tried to throw his weight in the opposite direction, and then he tried to kick her.

"STOP it, Gabriel, stop it RIGHT NOW!" Angie said, and

she could hear the hysteria in her voice.

Gabriel kept screaming. At the car he was still kicking and screaming, and there was no way she was going to be able to get him to lie down on the seat so she could change him, and when she tried to just buckle him into his car seat, he arched his back and shrieked until his face turned purple.

She was overwhelmed with panic and hopelessness, and suddenly she felt screams rising in her own throat to answer his, and she was even more terrified, because these screams were very, *very* big—bigger than herself or her ability to control them and if she actually screamed them she knew she would never be able to stop.

Then she felt herself go into some kind of altered state. Zombielike, she managed to pin Gabriel into the seat, and drive off in the car that was filled with the sound of his wailing and the smell of his poop, and keep driving, with no sense of purpose or direction, through a surreal landscape of gas stations and strip malls she vaguely remembered having seen maybe a hundred years ago. At some point, Gabriel stopped screaming and began to look over at her anxiously, saying, "Talk to me, Mommy. Mommy, please talk to me," but Angie heard him as though across a very large distance and she could not force herself to reply.

Eventually, she found herself in a parking lot in front of a store that looked as though it might be the store where her mother worked, and she carefully extracted Gabriel, now limp with exhaustion and anxiety, from the car seat, and carried him across the parking lot, feeling each step as gigantic, as though she were trying to cross the surface of the moon. Her mom smiled at her and held out her arms, and then Angie saw something else register on her mother's face, and then Gabriel was in her mother's lap and her mother was yelling into the telephone, "He's in a meeting? Well, tell him this is an emergency and get him out of the meeting and tell him to call this number right away." And then Jeff was not on his way to Atlanta, he was on his way to take her to the hospital where her mother's psychiatrist practiced.

And Angie seized at a thin thread of hope, because, after all, she still had kept that very big scream from coming out of her mouth, and yet this time everyone had been made to hear her, and now finally she was going to get the help she needed.

◈

But then, at the hospital, she came back to reality. The doctor was offering to admit her, and part of her really wanted that. But then she heard the doctor asking Jeff, "Do you think she's the type to dramatize something to get attention?" and she thought: "He doesn't have a clue what's going on with me." And suddenly it seemed very important to convince the doctor that she did not dramatize things, she was totally normal, totally in control, maybe a little strung out but not crazy like her mother.

So then she heard that calm, detached voice coming out of herself again, and they all had a very reasonable discussion about health plans and how treatment at that hospital would not be covered by Angie and Jeff's HMO. Jeff had that very scared, very humbled, very concerned look on his face, the look he got when he'd been brought back suddenly from somewhere he'd been soaring on his own. He was back! So she could trust him when he said he would stay home from work all that week with her, and take care of Gabriel, and help her make whatever calls she had to make to get some kind of treatment through the HMO.

And so they drove back to Westerville that evening in the Toyota, badly shaken, with the feeling that they had been severed from their old life in some major but as yet indefinable way. And they had totally forgotten about Nina when the phone rang the next morning at seven A.M. and she said breathlessly, "Today's the day, can you pick up Sam from day care at five if the baby's not born yet?" And since they couldn't possibly explain to her what had just happened, not understanding it themselves, they found themselves saying: "Sure."

Nina was still in labor at nine in the evening, so they ended up keeping Sam overnight. He woke up once, around two or three, crying for Nina, and Angie held him on the couch and rocked him gently. Odd, how strong she felt rocking him, this definite sense she had that she was the grown-up and he the baby, that it was within her power to calm him. Whereas when she rocked Gabriel, his sobs consumed her, his pain enveloped her, they became as one—hadn't they begun as one? Only then it had been the placid mother that contained them both, whereas now they were both contained within the howling baby.

◆

The HMO prescribed Prozac for Angie and told her to get a life.

"The relationship between a husband and a wife *always* changes after the birth of a child," said the therapist.

"Yeah, but not this much," Angie said. "You gotta understand, he used to bring me breakfast in bed."

The therapist just stared at her for a moment like that was some kind of non sequitur. Then she said, "Are you sure you're not jealous of his job? You say you used to be in the same field, and he's doing quite well for himself now."

"I'm *not* jealous of his job," Angie said. "I *hate* his job. I'd *never* work for a company like BDCC."

"Well," said the therapist, "but perhaps it would help to

find some sort of work that is personally meaningful for you. At least at this point you *know* that just being home all day with Gabriel doesn't seem to be helping you."

"She doesn't get it," Angie kept thinking. "She thinks I'm a bored little housewife with bored little housewife problems." But at some level, Angie, too, hoped that was the extent of it. If her problems were so close to the surface, then her deepening intuition that the foundations of her soul were completely rotted out might be wrong.

So she went back to the Y and signed Gabriel up for three days of day care, and this time Jeff just accepted it, because he was scared. Then she went to the quilt store where she had taken lessons and got herself hired as a salesperson for the Christmas season. And at first it was just such a relief to work in a place where other grown-ups came and you smiled at them and said, "How are you today?" and rang things up on the cash register. And then, after six weeks, the Prozac kicked in, and she felt much better all the time.

For about a month. But just before Christmas, she went into another nosedive. The store was boring. Jeff, who now clearly believed the crisis had passed, had reverted to his old withdrawn self. Playgroup meetings had become completely intolerable, because Gabriel always got into a conflict with someone and at the first sign of that Angie would start to fall apart. She didn't even want to see Grace or Nina separately anymore; it was like talking to the HMO shrink, they sort of assumed her problems were on their level—manageable. When she looked out the window the neighboring apartment buildings seemed to squeeze in on her, cutting into her supply of oxygen.

"Jeff," she said one night, after Gabriel had gone to bed. "We *gotta* work this out. I just can't live like this."

Jeff looked at her, not with his usual tight, irritated look, but kind of sadly. "Angie, we keep talking about it and talking about it, and we never get anywhere. I don't see how we *can* work it out."

"I just want us to be a family," Angie said. "I just want us to *feel* like a family."

"I know you do," said Jeff. "I can totally understand it. It's just, I *can't* feel it. I never wanted kids. I still don't want kids. I just want to live alone with you somewhere, in our old life, and have that old you back."

"I know you do," said Angie. "Only, I don't feel like the old me anymore, and we can't get that life back."

They talked late into the night. She wanted him to come to therapy with her, but he flat-out refused. "I can't do it, Angie, I just can't. Who are those people anyway? Most of them are quacks, and you're paying them to do what a friend ought to do for you for free."

"But you don't *talk* to your friends, do you? Do you ever talk to Ellis about your *feelings*?"

"That's not the way men talk to each other. Listen, Angie, I'm not saying I don't have some messy shit inside me, but I'm not toting it out for some total stranger to judge for me."

So in the end, they decided to do what they had always de-cided to do before when one of their life-style fantasies had soured; they decided to move. They would go back to the western suburbs where they had lived for the year after Gabriel was born, where they could get a nice newer house with a washer and dryer. Out far enough where they could afford to buy, it would be a bitch of a commute for Jeff, maybe an hour and a half each way on the train. But it was really only fair (she got the baby he didn't want so he got the job she hated so she got the house in the suburbs that would make his commute inconvenient). "Are you sure you wouldn't mind that I'd get home that late?" Jeff kept asking, but Angie felt like, "You're hardly here anyway, how much difference could it make?"

She fell asleep, feeling they had finally made some real

progress, and she dreamed of a quiet dead-end street where all
the houses shared one huge backyard and all the kids played
there together all day long without fighting, while the women
leaned over one another's shrubs and traded vegetarian
recipes and complained about their absent husbands, who
came home and barbecued on the weekends, and were all
good-looking, and knew how to flirt.

They spent two Saturdays looking in Bubbling Stream and
bought the seventh house they saw, a 1950s three-bedroom
split-level with a big backyard.

Two days later, Jeff came home from work and announced,
"Listen, Angie, I think this is *the* project. They're sending Joe
Morton down to Phoenix to do this job, and they want me to
be the liaison with the client, and they're sending a bunch of
other Chicago people down there, too. So what do you
think?"

"How long?"

"About a year, probably."

"So what do we do with the new house?"

The people who lived there now were retiring, and hadn't
seemed in any big hurry to vacate. Jeff proposed they offer to
let them rent it for another year.

"Well, if we can work that out, then I guess it's okay,"
Angie said. (She had gotten the house in the suburbs that
would make his commute inconvenient, so he should get the
transfer.)

The next day he came home and said, "Joe Morton's going
down there tomorrow, and they want me to go the day after
that."

"What about me and Gabriel?"

"They'll fly you down as soon as the contract for the project is signed, and they're saying that should be about a week."

So two days later, Jeff was gone, and Angie was quitting the quilt store job and pulling Gabriel out of day care and dragging cartons back to the apartment, and they were moving to Phoenix. Just like that.

◈

Only it wasn't just like that. At the end of the first week, Jeff said they thought it would take another week to get the contract signed, and at the end of the second week, he said no one was sure when the contract would get signed. Meanwhile, Angie was alone with Gabriel all day, leading a kind of suspended life, waiting for the call to go, and the days were long and horrible, but the nights were even worse. During the day she consoled herself with fantasies of life in Phoenix that were like her fantasies of life in Bubbling Stream, only here it was slushy, frigid January, and in Arizona it would be summertime and everybody had swimming pools, at least that's what Jeff had said. But at night awful thoughts crept into her fantasies. She couldn't sleep. She wasn't safe. She heard the creaks and groans of the old Westerville apartment building, and she thought of the guy downstairs who said stuff to her like, "Oh, you have such a beautiful smile," like you're supposed to take that as a compliment, but you know they really mean it as an insult, like who asked *them* for their opinion, and when a guy you're just trying to be basically friendly to starts saying stuff like that, it's really a threat. Could this guy find out that Jeff wasn't here? His door was right at the bottom of the stairs, he might keep track of stuff like that, he was always hanging around with nothing better to do, he was always inviting her out for coffee and she knew he really wanted her, he had this really creepy look in his eye.

Every night the fear of that guy got worse and worse, until Angie was convinced it was just a matter of time until he finally did come up after her, and in the middle of one night, in a fit of pure terror so bad she wanted to pull all the blankets up over her head, she forced herself to run down the hall to Gabriel's room and scooped him up in her arms and pulled jackets around both of them and then, as quickly and as quietly as she could, carried him tiptoe down the stairs past the guy's door and out to the car, and then she drove to her parents' bungalow and rang the doorbell over and over.

Her father appeared in the doorway in his pajamas. "Hi," he said, as though this were normal—although after all these years with her suicidal mother, how could he tell what was normal?—and Angie said, "I just got a little scared out there in Westerville all by myself; I was wondering if we could stay here tonight," and her dad said, "Fine."

So then they all decided she should stay there until things got straightened out in Phoenix. And Jeff kept telling her, "They charge your airfare to the client, that's why we've got to wait for the contract," and she was trying to be patient.

One evening her mom took her and Gabriel to Party Pizza, one of those huge restaurants they have in the suburbs that's basically a miniature amusement park for kids. Gabriel loved the place, so it was a big treat for him, and a little time off for Angie. After a while, Angie heard somebody crying and it sounded like Gabriel, but every kid sounds like your kid in a place like that. But it made her realize she hadn't seen him in a while, so she went looking for him and she couldn't find him anywhere, and as she got closer to the playhouse the crying got louder and she was sure it *was* him, and then she got close enough to peek through the window and see him. He was lying on the floor bawling, and two kids younger than him but bigger were standing on top of him, holding him down, and one of them was grabbing big handfuls of his hair and yanking them right out of his head, and his head was bleeding bad enough to make your stomach churn.

"You little SHITS," spat Angie, going at them like a kamikaze bomber. The boy got away from her, but she dragged the little girl over to her mother along with the wailing Gabriel and showed her his bloody bald patch, and the mother got real upset and started yelling at the girl in this shaky voice, and then Angie carried Gabriel, still crying, all around the restaurant until she found the little boy, but *his* mother just looked at her real mean and said, "Yeah, well that kinda stuff happens in here a lot; maybe you oughta keep a better eye on your kid," and Angie just stood there, totally speechless, feeling like if she had a gun she would *murder* this woman. And all around her kids were laughing and yelling and the video games were beeping and dinging. Angie's stomach was turning inside out and so was her head. Where the fuck was Jeff? The moms spent hours and hours in the Tot Lot teaching their kids not to hit, not to hit back. Wasn't this why they fucking stayed home in the first place? To make sure the kids were all properly socialized and peaceful and nonviolent and loving? But you know, what you want when something like this happens to your kid is for him to punch his fucking way out of there. And isn't that something his goddamn father should have taught him?

At her mother's house, Angie dialed Phoenix and told Jeff, "We're getting on a plane tomorrow."

"Now wait a minute, Angie, are you sure you can't wait a couple of days? You get a much better deal on an advance-purchase ticket, and if the contract never gets signed, we're going to have to eat this fare ourselves."

"Jeff," said Angie, "I am coming down TOMORROW."

IN THE KITCHEN

So here we are, back at the end of the story, and the beginning: in Angie's kitchen, wedging cheese graters and Tupperware canisters into the corners of packing cartons. We keep up a kind of desultory chatter, designed to distract Angie from the thought of where she is going, and also to distract ourselves from the great summing up that this evening has the potential to be. Are we emptier now or fuller than when we first met? We know, all three of us, privately, that our friendships have fallen short of our initial fantasies. Grace has not asked Angie to be present at the home birth of her baby, an idea Angie would once have thought of as "cool" but of which she now seems to bitterly disapprove (and Grace knows this without needing to be told). Angie is not expecting to miss us as much as two years of day-to-day friendship might suggest; her neediness now is like a bomb in the process of detonation, nothing Grace and I could ever even begin to dismantle. And Grace and I will not be brought together by Angie's departure; we will remain at arm's length over mutual suspicion of the other's disapproval, not to mention Grace's own impending departure from Westerville late in summer, after the new baby is a manageable age and Michael has finally finished his dissertation.

Grace, obviously preoccupied, begins quizzing me about my childbirth experience with the midwife. I emphasize the positive.

"I'll tell you what was really great," I say. "When the pain got really bad, I started to scream, like I did the first time. Only the first time, they just kept offering me more drugs and standing around looking like they wished I would shut up. And what Leonora did was she took both my hands and looked right into my eyes and said, 'Nina, you have to make that scream work for you.' And then she started grunting with me, making this sound that came from deep inside her belly instead of from her throat, like, 'UNNGH, UNNGH, UN-NGH.' And she was right, it was like finding another muscle deep inside me that helped me push. UNNGH, UNNGH, UNNGH," I went, hamming it up a little to get them both smiling. But then I couldn't resist adding, for the benefit of Grace, who was planning to have three-year-old Phoebe witness the birth, "I'm not sure, though, that it was anything I would've wanted Sam to hear me going through."

Grace heard the judgment. For a moment she just sat back in her seat, her hands resting on the peak of her great belly. Then she addressed Angie.

"Do you remember, Angie, one of the first conversations we had, when I had just told you my childbirth story, and then you asked me *why* I thought that had happened to me? That there must have been some element of spiritual growth in it that maybe I wasn't ready yet to see?"

"Yeah," said Angie tiredly. "I was such a wise old optimist then."

"But there really *was* something," Grace said, "and I finally realized what it was. All those ideas I had before I had Phoebe, about control and morality. Like if you just worked hard and did all the right things and ate all the right foods, you could control the kind of childbirth you would have. That you could control the kind of parenting experience you would have, that women who sent their kids to day care were bad mothers, and women who stayed home with their kids could produce exactly the kind of kid they wanted as long as they believed in the right philosophy—that's what the lesson of that birth was for me: not to think I could control all my

THE PLAYGROUP 197

experiences, and not to judge anyone else for making a choice
that was different from my own."

◈

Well, there's a nice booklike ending for you. It brings out a
crucial point: that no matter how many female stories we in-
vent to replace the old male ones, we will never agree on what
the plots ought to be; and we will not be able to shop for
them, off-the-rack, and expect them to fit the unique requirements of our individual lives.

I only wish it were true that Grace had learned this lesson
in the way book people do, but real-life people don't: not once
and for all, with no backsliding. It would be nice to report
that she woke up every morning after that night in the
kitchen a nonjudgmental human being at one with the universe. . . . But it is perhaps safer to say that she had glimpsed
an elusive truth that she was then able to summon up for
comfort in the really, really bad moments of Motherhood,
when that other "truth"—the one we learn in expensive, elite
institutions of higher education, and through our media, and
through the teachings of the myriad political isms and the
various childbirth sects—the truth that says we *do* control
our destinies, we *are* free to make the choices that determine
the quality of our lives—rings so surprisingly, bitterly hollow.

She was able to cling to it the very next very long day,
when she finally went into labor with her second baby, when
the first hour of the pushing was incredibly hard and painful,
and then the second hour of pushing was incredibly hard and
painful, and then the third hour of pushing was incredibly
hard and painful, and by the fourth hour, the midwife and the
home birth doctor and Michael and Grace's brother Gerald
were all standing around looking glum and no one was shout-

ing "PUSH" anymore. Then she began to lose her grasp of it, except for the moments when Gerald brought Phoebe into the room, and Phoebe approached the bed and said very gently, "How you doing, Mama?" and touched Grace's forehead and murmured, "Don't worry, Mama, it will be all right."

And truthfully, she lost it—lost it completely—as the hours of pushing continued to wear on and the big contractions kept ripping through her, and even she who had wanted this home birth so desperately began to wonder why they weren't taking her to the hospital by now, surely no one could keep enduring this kind of pain, please couldn't they just give her an epidural or a cesarean or *anything* that would just stop it, but if *this* was bad, imagine trying to walk, imagine trying to ride in a car going BUMP BUMP BUMP to the hospital, and it was just like that mountain in Kyoto on their honeymoon, the sweat pouring out of them and the sun beating down on them and the water gone.

But, look: Childbirth, unlike Motherhood, is always a story. It has an inherent plot, a beginning, a middle, and an end. It is never an unfinished art; no matter how stuck you feel in the middle, you have no choice but to move forward toward the conclusion. And, unlike Motherhood, with its rambling, incoherent drone that drives away bystanders, the birth story generates tremendous enthusiasm in other adults, who want to participate, to help push push push the story through to its anticipated happy ending.

So eventually the doctor's big bearlike partner, who heads the practice, is standing there filling up the doorway, booming, "Oh, this is going so WELL! There's no question this baby's going to come ANY MINUTE!" And then everyone is reenergized, and the chanting "PUSH" begins again and carries her through the sixth hour and the seventh, and finally there is a terrible, unbearable burning at her opening and then an immediate relief, and Phoebe is jumping up and down and the cork pops off a bottle of champagne and Michael is telling her it's a girl and the bearish doctor is standing there with tears streaming down his cheeks, saying, "I used to cry at every birth, but now I only cry at the special ones."

And although every muscle in her body is so thoroughly exhausted and sore that Grace cannot walk for three days afterward, she is ecstatic about this birth. Once we are not stuck in the story, in the pain of the unfinished work, we can look back and see how well worth it it was, in bringing about its ending. This time, Grace has gotten the birth she wanted: the baby nursing, still warm and wet from her womb; her family gathered round her; the safety of a place she trusts. So even though it isn't strictly, literally true that she has learned this lesson about lack of control—even though she has never really been able to fathom the unfairness of that first birth, or rearrange it satisfactorily in her self-esteem—this second birth, this triumph, erases it somewhat and heals it, ends it, so that she can, in some small way, begin her Motherhood again.

◆

For Angie, this move, this new beginning, turns out also to be the end of an old, unfinished story. It takes only a few weeks in the withering heat of Phoenix, in the neutrally decorated condo in the middle of an endless series of strip malls, with no friends or support network of any kind, and full-time responsibility for Gabriel, before the very, very, big scream inside her finally comes out, before Jeff responds to another emergency phone call to find her locked in the bedroom, away from Gabriel, chanting fiercely to herself, "Just hold on till help comes."

She spends several months at a psychiatric hospital, where,

on the first day, they hand her a photocopy of the weekly schedule, and she can see it all laid out for her—no decisions, no choices—and the great beauty of it is that, there on the paper, the weeks divided vertically into days, the days divided horizontally into hours, life becomes a quilt. Each hour a square with its own pattern, its own activity: group therapy, art therapy, occupational therapy, individual therapy, breakfast, lunch, dinner, relaxation, bedtime. No unstructured time here, and any project you start they make you finish, and not only do they listen to your every whisper, they force out of you the things you didn't want to say, the things you had to keep inside because they were so vile, the things that were ripping the fabric of your self apart; the voice. And they make you get up every single morning and stitch the squares together, one after another—the craft before the art—until the days add up to weeks, and the weeks to months, and they teach you in this way that even a work in progress has a certain pattern and direction, wherein lie both its security and all of its potential for creativity.

◆

And then there was me. I am the one who just can't learn the lesson, who can't accept the idea of the unfinished work or the life that, plotless, is essentially beyond control. My life is structured around this writing, which will add up to something concrete, the thing I have grown up believing is more real than life itself: a book. The children are not what I Do. They simply grow up like grass, with watering and some care on my part. I cannot measure my value by their existence; yet their existence was the main catalyst in my understanding that the way I measured my life was wrong.

The point was not for me to become successful, although

for a while after the playgroup broke up I had the opportunity to feel I was. When my first book was published, I went off on a little book tour to publicize my thesis: that Motherhood is not what the books and magazines say it is—the clichés of the Homemaker and the Supermom—but a great deal messier. And in TV and newspaper interviews they cleaned up all the messiness, rouged my cheekbones, and presented me as the very living example of the thing I was arguing doesn't exist: *She writes, she raises kids, she comes on this show . . . she must be—SUPERWOMAN!*

To be without a voice, it seems, is to be a homemaker, a mere mother; to be with a voice is to be Superwoman (a woman who talks like a man, and "more of a man each day"). There is some middle ground that we are just discovering—to speak in the voice of a woman—but we must be careful about the way we do it, lest we be dismissed, à la Judy Chicago, as both unmanly and unladylike in either our medium or our message or both.

It is only because I stumbled blindly out of the library one day and impulsively had a baby that I discovered this place where voices do not expect to be heard, trees routinely falling in forests where no one comes to listen—except the other like voices, trapped in the same circumstance of Motherhood. And that is what Grace, Angie, and I did for one another in those two years: In the murky, unmanly part of life, where the stories have no endings, where the works are eternally in progress, where a person could lose all sense of direction, we tried to be one another's midwives, holding one another's hands, suggesting ways we might be able to make our screams work for us, reminding one another when to push—but mostly listening to one another, day by day, and in listening, creating the structure, and the plot. (And in the way of life, rather than of books, of course only partially succeeding.)

NOTES

IN THE KITCHEN

GENERAL SOURCES

Mary Catherine Bateson, *Composing a Life*, Plume/Penguin, New York, 1990.

Carolyn G. Heilbrun, *Writing a Woman's Life*, Ballantine Books, New York, 1989.

NOTES

14 "the individual effort . . .": Bateson, op. cit., p. 18.

CHAPTER 1: CHILDBIRTH STORY: GRACE

GENERAL SOURCES

Suzanne Arms, *Immaculate Deception: A New Look at Women and Childbirth in America*, San Francisco Book Company/Houghton Mifflin, Boston, 1975.

Robert A. Bradley, *Husband-Coached Childbirth*, 3rd. ed., Harper & Row, New York, 1981.

Andrea Dworkin, *Woman Hating: A Radical Look at Sexuality*, Plume/NAL-Dutton, New York, 1991.

Frances Moore Lappé, *Diet for a Small Planet*, rev. ed., Ballantine Books, New York, 1982.

Susan McCutcheon-Rosegg, with Peter Rosegg, *Natural Childbirth the Bradley Way*, Plume/Penguin, New York, 1984.

NOTES

17 "There is no doubt": Arms, op. cit., p. 21.

17 "I can promise": McCutcheon-Rosegg, op. cit., p. 97.

20 "[T]he only way": Lappé, op. cit., p. 25.

21 "Mother would remove": Howard S. Levy, *Chinese Footbinding: The History of a Curious Erotic Custom*, W. Rawls, New York, 1966, pp. 26–28. Quoted in Dworkin, op. cit., p 100. Italics mine.

24 "When you are in labor": McCutcheon-Rosegg, op. cit., p. 59.

24 "prefer to have": Ibid., p. 21. Italics mine.

24 "the difference between": Bradley, op. cit., p. 11.

26 "The medicated mothers": Ibid., p. 29.

26 "The drugged mothers'": Ibid., pp. 18–19.

31 "second-rate copy": McCutcheon-Rosegg, op. cit., p. 214.

32 "You are examined": Ibid., p. 171.

33 "The list": Ibid., p. 199.

35 "The length of time": Bradley, op. cit., p. 23.

37 "In the Bradley": McCutcheon-Rosegg, op. cit., p. 8.

CHAPTER 2: MIND-BODY STORY: NINA

GENERAL SOURCES

Judy Chicago, *The Birth Project*, Doubleday, New York, 1985.

George Gilder, *Men and Marriage*, rev. ed. of *Sexual Suicide* [1973], Pelican Publishing Co., Gretna, 1986.

Carolyn G. Heilbrun, *Writing a Woman's Life*, Ballantine Books, New York, 1989.

Elaine Morgan, *The Descent of Woman*, Stein & Day, New York, 1972.

Desmond Morris, *The Naked Ape: A Zoologist's Study of the Human Animal*, McGraw-Hill, New York, 1967.

NOTES

53 "For women who wish": Heilbrun, op. cit., p. 48.

70 "There is no distinctly": Mark Twain, *Pudd'nhead Wilson. Pudd'nhead Wilson's New Calendar*, quoted in John Bartlett, *Familiar Quotations*, 15th ed., Little Brown and Co., Boston, 1980.

72 Judy Chicago's account of working on "The Birth Project" appears in her book by the same name, op. cit., in the Introduction, pp. 4–7, and the Afterword, pp. 224–25.

CHAPTER 3: MARRIAGE STORY: ANGIE

GENERAL SOURCES

Robert Coles, *Dorothy Day: A Radical Devotion*, Addison-Wesley, Boston, 1987.

Robert Ellsberg, ed., *By Little and By Little: The Selected Writings of Dorothy Day*, Knopf, New York, 1983.

Betty Friedan, *The Feminine Mystique*, 20th anniversary ed., Laurel/Dell, New York, 1983.

Lynne Sharon Schwartz, *Disturbances in the Field*, Bantam Books, New York, 1985.

NOTES
79 "[A] novel,": Schwartz, op. cit., p. 112.

CHAPTER 4: PARENTING STORY: GRACE

GENERAL SOURCES
John Bradshaw, *Homecoming: Reclaiming and Championing Your Inner Child*, Bantam Books, New York, 1990.

Ushanda io Elima, "Life with the Pygmies," *Mothering* magazine, Summer 1988, pp. 89–95.

Betty Friedan, *The Feminine Mystique*, 20th anniversary ed., Laurel/Dell, New York, 1983.

NOTES
119 "[Middle-class mothers]": Sociologist Arnold Green, quoted in Friedan, op. cit., p. 201.

119 "[W]hen a child's development": Bradshaw, op. cit., p. 7.

119 "The Pygmies": Elima, op. cit.

120 "During [the first] year": Elima, op. cit.

123 "The [Pygmy] father": Ibid.

130 "[Pygmies] are not afraid": Ibid.

133 "Hallet never saw": Ibid.

CHAPTER 5: CAREER STORY: NINA

GENERAL SOURCES
Mary Catherine Bateson, *Composing a Life*, Plume/Penguin, New York, 1990.

Barbara Kantrowitz with Pat Wingert and Kate Robins, "Advocating a 'Mommy Track,'" *Newsweek*, March 13, 1989, p. 45.

Phyllis Schneider, "The Managerial Mother," *Working Woman*, December 1987, pp. 117–32.

NOTES
147 "Women's lives offer": Bateson, op. cit., p. 184.

147 "The new managerial mother": Schneider, op. cit.

148 "There is no question": Ibid.

149 "Managerial mothers are": Ibid.

152 "When Matthew was born": Ibid.

157 "[Managerial couples] go": Ibid.

170 "Without a strategy": Kantrowitz, op. cit. Italics mine.

170 "Usually menstruate together": Ushanda io Elima, "Life with the Pygmies," *Mothering* magazine, Summer 1988, p. 89.

CHAPTER 6: VOICE STORY: ANGIE

GENERAL SOURCES

Betty Friedan, *The Feminine Mystique*, 20th anniversary ed., Laurel/Dell, New York, 1983.

NOTES

175 "It is frightening": Friedan, op. cit., p. 338.